Shooting Star

Shooting Star

The Colin Stein Story

COLIN STEIN

WITH PAUL SMITH

BIRLINN

First published in 2009 by
Birlinn Limited
West Newington House
10 Newington Road
Edinburgh
EH9 1QS

www.birlinn.co.uk

ISBN: 978 1 84158 838 4

British Library Cataloguing-in-Publication Data
A catalogue record for this book is available from the British Library

Typeset by Iolaire Typesetting, Newtonmore
Printed and bound by MPG Books Ltd, Bodmin

To my wife, Linda, and our wonderful children and grandchildren

Contents

1

The thrill of the chase

'We would like you to sign for Rangers.' Those are the eight words that changed my life forever. I had walked into an Edinburgh hotel as a humble wee boy from Philpstoun and strode out just a few hours later with my heart pounding, chest puffed out and feeling 10 feet tall. I had just become part of The Rangers Football Club and it felt like a truly unbelievable moment.

When I signed for the club that had been home to my childhood heroes, I was still just a young lad trying to make his way in the game and in life. I joined in 1968, not knowing what lay in front of me or what path my life would follow. What I did know was that one of the dreams I had held so dear since I was a schoolboy had just come true.

Rangers invested heavily to take me from Hibernian to Ibrox and broke all sorts of records to make it happen. I became the subject of the first £100,000 transfer between Scottish clubs, the most expensive player ever recruited by Rangers and the most valuable asset ever sold by the Easter Road board.

You would have thought that might put a lot of pressure on such young shoulders, but none of that mattered to me. What was important was getting my hands on that light blue jersey and proving I had what it took to become a Rangers player in the mould of those I had grown up idolising.

I was just 21-years old when Rangers wrote that six-figure cheque and the move to Ibrox was another dramatic development in a career that was progressing unexpectedly swiftly. Just three years earlier, I had been holding down a day job and playing junior football, and there I was putting pen to paper on a contract with one of the biggest clubs in the world for the largest fee they had ever paid.

I had been a late developer in football terms, not even playing as a striker until my late teens, but from playing my first game as a forward with junior side Armadale to signing my first professional contract with Hibernian took less than one year.

I never envisaged the way my life would unfold and could not have foreseen the drama that would follow my arrival at Ibrox. There was joy and sadness, success and frustration, as well as no end of excitement in more than a decade in light blue, but simply making it to Ibrox in the first place was one of the biggest challenges I faced.

If the Easter Road board had had their way, I would never have sat in the home dressing room at Ibrox and, more importantly as far as they were concerned, I would never have lined up against the team I was leaving behind in Leith.

Fortunately for me, Rangers were well versed in boxing clever when it came to bouts in the transfer market and after patiently biding their time, they landed the killer blow on 31 October 1968. That was the day the dream I had held since I first started kicking a ball around came true, a day I will never forget.

Nor will I ever forget the game of cat and mouse that led up to it. I had been at Hibs for three years when the murmurs about interest from other clubs first began to start, a few months into the 1968/69 season. It is impossible not to take notice of what is being said about you; after all, it is your future that's being discussed. I soon found it is difficult to know which Chinese whispers to believe and which to discount, even when you're at the centre of it all. The strong tip was that West Ham were ready to make a bid and Rangers were also said to be interested. I had no way of knowing whether the Londoners were waiting in the wings, but I could be confident about the Ibrox link.

What nobody knew as the drama began to unfold was that I'd had word from Rangers, or a hint at least, that they wanted to sign me. That bit of advance notice gave me an edge during a fraught and hectic period that would define my life.

Had the Ibrox manager Davie White not tipped me the wink, I may well have been whisked away from Scotland before even knowing that Rangers were keen. Technically he hadn't broken any regulations, all he did was take me aside and tell me he was a big admirer of me as a player. There's nothing wrong in that, as far as I know it has never been illegal to pay someone a compliment, but I read between the lines and from that point on was confident the call would eventually come.

I later discovered that Sunderland were also ready to weigh in with a big offer and there's no doubt that south of the border is where the directors at Hibs wanted me to go. I, on the other hand, had my heart set on something a little closer to home. The west coast was as far as I needed to go.

The rumour and speculation began to have an impact on me. Any player who says uncertainty doesn't affect them isn't being honest; it's only natural to want things settled one way or another and I had reached that point as winter approached. It was becoming obvious that both the club and I had a decision to make on my future and with no resolution on the horizon, I decided to force their hand by putting in a transfer request. It wasn't a popular decision down in Leith but, for all they claimed they wanted me to stay, I do think it suited the club to sell to the highest bidder.

The main frustration for me was that I just couldn't see a way of winning trophies with Hibs. We had great players and a wonderful manager, but behind it all there was an inferiority complex that extended to all of the provincial clubs. There wasn't really the belief that the Old Firm could be toppled and I found that difficult. Off the park, I was easy-going and relaxed, but when I crossed the white line something else took over, I became a different person. That will to win got me in hot water more than once, but it was a big part of making me the player I was. Over time, I realised I would have to move on if I was going to satisfy the craving I had for success. I didn't feel guilty about it, because Hibs had bought me for practically nothing and stood to make a very healthy return.

It all came to a head one afternoon when the Hibs chairman, William Harrower, greeted me after training and informed me I'd be going with him to the Caledonian Hotel at the top of Princes Street for transfer talks. I was told that the deal had been agreed between the clubs and all that was left to do was for me to finalise my side of it. What I wasn't told was who the buyer was.

Harrower was an Edinburgh bookmaker, big in business yet relatively new in football terms, having only taken over as the top man at Easter Road a few years earlier. The old adage about there being no such thing as a poor bookie rang true and his reign at Hibs coincided with a new wave of money flowing around the club. That doesn't mean Harrower was reckless, far from it. He was a businessman first and foremost and always drove a hard bargain, particularly when it came to wheeling and dealing in the transfer market. Before long, he sold out to Tom Hart, who had made his money in house-building and development, but he certainly enjoyed an eventful time in charge of the club and brought in more than he spent.

I had absolutely no idea who was waiting for me at the hotel when Harrower and I set off on the short journey to the city centre meeting but I was hoping and wishing that it would be Davie White and a Rangers contract. The chairman gave the game away as we climbed the steps leading to the front door. Quite matter of fact, he turned and told me that he would never let me sign for another Scottish club. There was no malice, no venom, but there was no doubt that he meant what he said. Hibs didn't want me coming back to haunt them and I could understand where they were coming from, but at the same time I was never one to be dictated to. If anything, that brief little exchange on Princes Street strengthened my resolve to do what was best for me and me alone. Whoever was ready to meet me had a battle on their hands to persuade me to sign, even before we had been introduced.

Waiting in a room deep inside the Caley was a man I recognised instantly: Harry Catterick. The Everton manager was one of the most respected men in the English game and he had assembled a team at Goodison Park that was packed full of household names. Joe Royle was the big star, but there was World Cup winner Alan Ball pulling the strings behind him and a long list of tremendous players in the mix including John Hurst, Jimmy Husband and Howard Kendall. Everton, who had won the FA Cup a couple of seasons earlier and the league title at the beginning of Catterick's spell in charge, had finished just six points off the pace when Manchester City won the championship the previous season. They were mounting another strong challenge when Catterick diverted north to try to tempt me to join them, chasing hard on the heels of a Leeds side which went on to win the title that term. Who knows if the positions would have been reversed had I decided to make the move, but Catterick obviously felt I could improve his side.

It was flattering that he wanted to sign me for Everton and we were locked in that room for hours as he tried to persuade me that my future lay south of the border. The Everton boss had a reputation as a stubborn and fierce character, one who liked to lay down the law. Those traits came through in our negotiations as he refused to give up without a fight. He assured me I'd be a first-team regular and praised me to the hilt, but I wasn't convinced.

For one thing, I'd never ventured away from my home village of Philpstoun in West Lothian and the prospect of upping sticks and moving to Merseyside was a daunting one. For another, I held the trump card of knowing that Rangers were ready to pounce, and that was the move I had my heart set on.

Everton would not take no for an answer and even sent a driver to collect my fiancée Linda from her work and ferry her back to the hotel to join the discussions.

There was a very attractive offer on the table, one that would set us up perfectly, and they obviously felt that if they could persuade Linda that Goodison was the right option then they would be halfway there. What they hadn't bargained for was the two of us standing firm in the face of pressure from both Hibs and Everton, with Linda making it clear she would support whatever choice I made. The money Everton were talking about was life-changing, figures beyond all of our expectations as well as the lure of a house and all sorts of other incentives, but no amount would have swayed me. After a lengthy meeting, Everton had to admit it was a losing battle and Catterick left to make his way back to the north-west of England empty-handed. In the end, he set me a two-hour ultimatum and when the clock ran down, he got the answer he didn't want and probably didn't expect.

It was either brave or foolish to turn down such a fantastic opportunity and within a day I was to discover which. The newspapers were plastered with stories about my imminent departure, but most were second-guessing what was about to happen. Obviously, news of Everton's attempt to sign me was doing the rounds, but the better informed among the media pack were hinting more and more strongly about interest from Rangers.

When I went into training the day after the Everton talks, I found myself firmly in the firing line. Teammates were lining up to rib me about my decision to say no to the type of offer they would have walked over hot coals for. It was all good fun, but I don't think they, or I, realised it would be the last they would see of me in Hibs gear. The next day, I was working with a new set of players.

Nobody from the Hibs board or the manager spoke to me that morning. They were smarting from my decision to reject Everton and gave me the cold shoulder. After training, I went up the road to Waverley Station to catch my train back to Linlithgow and I was cornered on the platform by a couple of reporters. It was the press who told me that Hibs had accepted an offer from Rangers and I would be free to speak to them, not the club themselves. I didn't really know what to believe, because the silence from Easter Road was deafening.

I decided just to head for home, but it was a restless journey. The train rolled into Linlithgow and I headed for the house. I was settling down at home for the afternoon when there was a knock at the door. Standing on my doorstep was a driver sent by Rangers to take me back into Edinburgh for talks. The trip from Philpstoun to the capital is all of 20 miles but it felt like the longest journey of my life. Every possible scenario was running through my head and the excitement was tinged with fear. What if it didn't work out the way I hoped? It didn't bear thinking about.

Eventually, the car drew to a halt opposite Edinburgh Zoo at a modest hotel, where a big gleaming Bentley was parked conspicuously outside. I was ushered in and found two familiar faces waiting for me. The first was Davie White and the second was the Rangers vice-chairman Matt Taylor, which explained the Bentley. Taylor later succeeded John Lawrence as chairman and was well suited to the positions of power he held, being impeccably turned out and with a quiet air of authority that befitted his standing in the game.

Without any small talk, Davie White said then and there that Rangers wanted me to sign. I was told that a fee between the clubs had been agreed, but at no point was the actual figure quoted to me. Instead, we spoke about my side of the bargain, with both White and Taylor doing their bit to sell the club to me. They needn't have bothered, since my mind had been made up from the moment I got in the car that afternoon. There was no real negotiation on my part, certainly no agent playing piggy in the middle, and it took little more than an hour for us to finalise the details of what proved to be a landmark transfer in Scottish football. The package Everton had offered was fantastic but, to their credit, Rangers matched it pound for pound. There was a big misconception at the time that I would have been far better off financially by going to England, but I was well looked after.

There was no medical carried out by Rangers and no second opinion for me to call on, quite astonishing on both counts I suppose, when you consider it was the biggest transfer Scottish football had ever seen. The fact of the matter was that the game-network in our country was like that of a village. If there had been any underlying problem with my fitness then Rangers would have known about it and equally if I was getting a raw deal, I would have been well aware. Both parties were happy so there was no need to delay and the formalities were completed in time for tea. I was ferried back home in the same club car that had collected me earlier in the day, the only difference being that for this journey I was a Rangers player and not a Hibs employee.

I headed straight for Linda's house to break the good news to her and it was a night of celebration for both her family and mine. There was a real sense of achievement and I was happy to be able to share it with so many people who had supported me along the way. They knew what it meant to me to sign for Rangers, and the realisation that it had finally happened was as strong for those around me as it was for me personally.

I was joining a club determined to claw the championship trophy back from Celtic, who had won it three times on the trot up to that point. Having come from Hibs, I knew how highly regarded Jock Stein was at Easter Road and he had quickly put his stamp on the Celtic team to take them on that successful run. But there was certainly no feeling of inferiority at Rangers, either within the staff or among the supporters. Celtic's margin of victory during their three title wins was two points in 1966, three points in 1967 and then two points again in 1968. That was not the mark of a dominant team, more a sign that Celtic had enjoyed the breaks that Rangers hadn't.

Given how closely run every title race had been in the three previous years, there was no reason for anyone at Ibrox to suspect that the tide would not turn quickly, and throughout my discussions with Davie White and Matt Taylor, the overriding feeling was that this was the season it would happen. The fact it had been a mixed start to the season was neither here nor there, with just eight games played in the First Division when I joined there was an awful long way still to go.

The week before my debut, Rangers lost 3–2 against Aberdeen at Ibrox, just a fortnight after losing 2–0 at St Johnstone, so there was certainly a sense of urgency in terms of getting back on track, but no panic in the ranks. For one thing, the club was awash with supremely talented players and where you find ability, you will, more often than not, find confidence. Sandy Jardine, John Greig, Ronnie McKinnon and Willie Johnston were just some of the Scotland internationals on the books at that time, while Kai Johansen and Orjan Persson added a continental flavour. Rangers had not been afraid to spend big in the years leading up to my arrival, with Davie Smith and Alex Ferguson among the major recruits and Alex MacDonald following not long after me in another significant transfer.

All the ingredients for success were there and Davie White's task was to pull them together. It was a massive assignment, but Davie gave the impression he was confident success was just around the corner. He was young but enthusiastic, having initially joined the club as assistant manager to Scot Symon. White had played for Clyde before stepping up to coach and manage the Bully Wee, not the traditional type of CV for a Rangers manager, but he was in the right place at the right time when Symon was dismissed at the tail-end of 1967. He was not fierce or overbearing, but it was difficult not to respect a man who had taken on one of management's toughest challenges and was prepared to meet it head-on.

He did things differently from any other manager the club had seen. He ditched the traditional collar and tie in favour of a tracksuit and joined in with training, something totally alien to the players who had served under Symon. He was bright and his methods were good, but I'm not sure if he ever really felt like he belonged. I found out after I joined that Davie had taken two months after his appointment to the top job to even sit in the manager's chair at Ibrox; he felt he had to prove he was worthy of the office before he actually put his feet under the desk.

He wanted to prove himself to the squad as well. I can only speak for myself, but the fact he had never been a Rangers player, or an international, did not even enter my mind. As far as I was concerned, you had to judge a person on the here and now. In Davie's case, I didn't doubt his ability as a coach, and that was what mattered.

The other important factor was Davie's enthusiasm for bringing me on board. He tried a couple of times before the signing went through and had to be patient. Instead of signing somebody else, he hung on until he got his man. For any player, it's a brilliant thing to know the manager is so determined to have you in his squad.

Davie's task was to build a team to bring the title back to Ibrox. Kilmarnock had won the league prior to Celtic's three in a row, so the championship trophy was long overdue, having last been at Ibrox in 1964. The pressure was on, but Rangers had the players with the class and experience to handle that. As far as we were concerned, it was a case of when, not if, Celtic could be overtaken. Little did we know just how long it would take and how many amazing twists and turns there would be along the way.

My job was to get the goals that would help turn the near misses into success. Alex Ferguson, Willie 'Bud' Johnston and Orjan Persson had been regular scorers the previous season but the manager still felt he needed an out-and-out striker who would break through the 20-goal-a-season barrier, a figure Fergie and Bud had just fallen short of. At a club like Rangers, you can never take your place in the team for granted, but it would be a foolish manager who spent £100,000 on a player not to put him in his team, and although I was never given assurances by Davie White that I would be going straight into the side, it was pretty obvious that I would be in at the deep end.

Having concluded the deal on the Thursday afternoon, I reported for my first day at work the following morning. Signing a piece of paper on a desk in Edinburgh is one thing, but walking down Edmiston Drive and through the front doors of Ibrox for the first time is wholly different. My stomach was churning when the door swung open and the enormity of what I had signed up to hit me when the marble staircase confronted me. There can be no more imposing welcome to a football stadium than at Ibrox, where the building simply oozes history and quality. From the moment you set foot inside, you become instantly aware of the standards expected of you and there's a common bond, a sense of purpose, linking everyone who is part of the Rangers family.

Davie White gave me a quick and unceremonious introduction to the rest of the squad, really nothing more was required. Everyone in that dressing room was a household name and they all had plenty of experience playing against me.

Some knew me better than others, not least Alex Ferguson. He was the man in possession of the no. 9 shirt the previous season, so in many ways had more to lose than most when I joined. I don't know if he felt threatened, but he certainly already had reason to dislike me given we had both been sent off earlier in the year for coming to blows when I was with Hibs. It was a typically tousy affair at Ibrox when we took the long walk together, only the second red card I'd ever received but one that was fresh in the memories of the Rangers fans when I joined in 1968. They certainly let me know what they thought of me that day, when they were most definitely on the side of Alex. It is amazing how you never hear a word of what's being said on the terraces when you're in the heat of battle, you just make out the general noise, but as soon as you come out of that zone you can pick up every sound. After being sent off, the Rangers supporters gave me pelters as I trudged towards the dressing rooms, let's just say my parentage was questioned by more than one or two in the crowd that day. It's a lonely old place to be when you're in that situation, not least when it is against a team with a group of fans as passionate as the Rangers followers.

Given that that controversial game was my last encounter with my new Rangers teammates, I could have been forgiven for being a bit nervous about landing in amongst them. Any fears were quickly blown away as I settled quickly into the squad, and was welcomed with open arms by everyone. I was handed a peg in the dressing room next to John Greig; whether deliberate or not, it certainly helped being a new boy under the wing of the captain.

Our day-to-day work was at the club's old Albion training ground, just a stone's throw from the ground, and I had a gentle introduction to life as a Rangers player. Because I'd joined late in the week, the workload was tapering off as the squad built towards the weekend's game at Arbroath and that gave me the chance to ease my way in with a few light sessions and a bounce game with the lads. By that time, I'd already played for the Scottish Football League side, which was an under-23 select, and through that I'd played alongside quite a few of my new club colleagues.

That helped me settle and I quickly struck up friendships which survive to this day. I roomed with Ronnie McKinnon, one of the players I'd had a good relationship with even before I arrived, having played against him so many times, and I found the spirit at the club encouraging. There was confidence without arrogance, belief without any major egos to contend with. It was up to me to prove myself in that company and I couldn't wait for the adventure to begin.

2

From boy to man

Walking through the front door at Ibrox as a Rangers player was something I never even dared to dream of when I started out in the game. Yes I had belief in my own ability, but there was no master plan in my mind. All I started with was a love of the game and a determination to make the most of my talent. I had no idea where that would take me, but I'm fortunate to be able to look back on my career with enormous satisfaction. I experienced some amazing highs and tremendous occasions, while collecting memories that will stay with me forever.

The only real regret is that my parents were unable to share those good times with me. My father died when I was 6 and my mother passed away when I was just 17, before I got my break as a professional player with Hibs. Everyone wants to make their parents proud and I have to admit to a sense of disappointment that they did not see what I made of myself. Whether it was running out at Wembley or scoring important goals for Rangers, it was something I was always conscious of.

Dad was a miner and mum worked in the whisky factory at Queensferry, near to our home village of Philpstoun in West Lothian, and I have always wondered what they would have made of the path my life took. I am sure they would have approved. I have very early memories of my father and I like to think that he still influenced my career. As far as I'm concerned, football is in the Stein genes, since my two brothers and I all played at a decent level. I can think of a few pairs of football brothers, but groups of three showing promise are a bit more unusual. Dad had played for Newtongrange Star and his love of the game obviously rubbed off on us.

I was the baby of the family, with my sisters Dorothy and Helen joined by my brothers Eric and Bobby. Eric, as the eldest of the boys, led the way as far as football was concerned and was a very talented player who represented Scotland at junior level.

There is no doubt in my mind that Eric would have gone on to be a star in the senior game, but he suffered a knee injury while playing for Broxburn Athletic in a junior game and was never the same again. It was a tackle by a certain Dave Mackay which caused the problems. Mackay, who had been farmed out to Newtongrange Star by Hearts, of course went on to play for Spurs and Scotland but Eric, who is 13 years older than me, unfortunately never had the chance to fulfil his undoubted potential. The fact that he was picked by the Scotland junior selectors when he was playing week in and week out against the likes of Mackay tells its own story.

Bobby had a seven-year start on me and was another major inspiration. By the time I was entering my teens, he had been snapped up by Raith Rovers, having served his football apprenticeship with Broxburn Athletic, just like Eric before him.

Going to watch Bobby at Stark's Park and hearing his stories about life with Raith was my first real experience of professional football, and in hindsight I would say it removed some of the mystique surrounding the game at that level. It was normal to have football at a good standard in the family and subconsciously that must have been a major advantage when I was setting off on my own journey. I was certainly never in awe of anyone when I stepped up to the same stage, and having an early grounding in the senior game through my brother's involvement was part of that.

Rovers were in the top flight, the old First Division, when Bobby joined in 1960 and were back there, after dropping down to the Second Division for a couple of seasons, when he left for Montrose in 1969. He made more than 200 appearances for

Raith and our paths eventually crossed, playing against each other on a few occasions to give the rest of the family a thorny dilemma over who to support. After serving Montrose, he played for East Stirling and was a very well regarded and talented player.

Both he and Eric were always there to encourage me and give me good advice. They were both half-backs, a position I played myself when I wasn't at full-back, and I learnt a lot from them. The most important thing they told me was to stick in and never to give up. It sounds simple, but having the right attitude is one of the biggest factors in determining which players succeed and which fall by the wayside. I worked with plenty of very good players who never made it as far as they should have done, but I had the right people around me to push me on.

Given that my brothers had both played for Broxburn Athletic, it would have seemed natural for me to follow in their footsteps, especially since I played for Broxburn Strollers in the juvenile leagues. It didn't work out that way and I ended up on trial with Linlithgow Rose, who decided I wasn't up to scratch.

Trials were very much a one-off, you had 90 minutes to prove you deserved to be signed. There was no training for a week before, you were just thrown in at the deep end and it was a case of sink or swim.

The junior scene in the Lothian area was very strong at that time, with Broxburn and Linlithgow, who won the Scottish Junior Cup in 1965, the major players. On the other side of the country, the likes of Irvine Meadow and Kirkintilloch Rob Roy led the challenge to our teams on the east coast. Crowds were good, certainly far greater than those watching Third Division matches now when it came to the big games, and there was the added spice of strong local rivalry.

Teams were full of players out to make their name. At that time, if you had any ambitions of playing senior football you had to sign for a junior club first to preserve your right to play at that level if it didn't work out on the bigger stage, so there was a steady flow of players back and forth between the junior and senior leagues.

You would find a lot of clubs, from the First Division down, farming out young players to junior teams and also scouring that level to pick up talent who hadn't been spotted yet. It's a great shame that junior football has gone the other way now, with teams packed with players who are on their way down rather than on the up, because so many youngsters are whisked away by the senior teams at such a young age.

In the 1960s, the clubs still had the pick of the best young players and it was Armadale Thistle who decided to give me my chance. I like to think I repaid the faith they showed in me, even although I spent just one season with the club before Hibs stepped in. Armadale had a good relationship with Hibernian at that time, and I wasn't the first to play for both clubs.

Joe Baker, who went on to become an England international, was at Armadale before me, having been farmed out by Hibs, and I can't imagine there are too many junior clubs who can boast of having blooded future forwards for both sides of the Auld Enemy.

Joe, who died in 2003, is actually one of the first players I can remember watching in the flesh. He averaged almost forty goals a season during his four years at Hibs in the late 1950s and early 1960s, so it's not surprising that he is one player who sticks in my mind from childhood. I would have been 14 by the time he left Easter Road to join Denis Law at Torino, and Joe was obviously big news at that time. I can still picture him in full flight, always willing to get stuck in against players far bigger than he was, and more often than not getting the better of them.

Hibs and Rangers were the teams I supported as a boy. There was no rhyme or reason for it, like a lot of football supporters I suppose I was just taken by the two teams and they got under my skin. Growing up in the countryside outside Edinburgh, I thought of Hibs as my local team and was able to see them when I could. It was different with Rangers, because I couldn't get to Ibrox to see them, so they were the team I had to follow from a distance. Going a few miles down the road to Linlithgow was a bit of an expedition in those days, so travelling to the other side of the country to Ibrox just wasn't an option. There wasn't a particular family link with Rangers, but from a very early age they became my team.

Instead of travelling through to Glasgow, I had to sneak glimpses of them when they were closer to home and one of my most vivid Rangers memories from those early days comes from Tynecastle, where I'd gone with my sister Helen's husband John to see them play Hearts. John is a Jambo and I was delighted to tag along to games with him, especially if Rangers were involved. The thing that sticks in my mind is being amazed by how far George Young could kick the old brown leather ball. He was a colossus of a man, captain of club and country, and even from the terraces you got a real feeling for how imposing he was. Just thinking back to the equipment in those days makes me shudder, heading one of those balls was no mean feat and the boots today are like slippers in comparison to those we wore. Yet George, a big bear of a man, made it look as though he was playing with a balloon, it was effortless to him because of his strength and balance. Mind you, it wasn't all about force. George could play too and it was a massive honour for me to meet him later in life, long after he had hung up his boots. He was a gentleman as well as a wonderful player and it is always nice when your heroes live up to your expectations.

While I was able to watch some of Scotland's big names, like most kids my age I was far more interested in playing the game. As far back as I can remember, I was always kicking a ball around and I grew up in a great environment in that respect. I had two older brothers to pester for a game, and we lived in a great little village with a football pitch just a stone's throw from the house. From dawn until dusk, I'd be playing football without a care in the world, and I've often thought that we country boys were spoilt. There weren't many of us in the village, but it had a tennis court at that time and a bowling club, which is still going strong.

Philpstoun is a tiny dot on the map, just a handful of houses spread over half a dozen roads in the Forth Valley. It hasn't changed an awful lot since I grew up there, a few more houses have sprung up but it has escaped the type of development that has swamped other parts of West Lothian and is still surrounded by the rolling fields that were our extended playground.

There was no school in Philpstoun, so we made the short journey through to Bridgend as primary kids and then Linlith-gow, still only a couple of miles away, when we were older. It was at school that I began to take football more seriously, getting my first taste of organised teams at secondary school and joining the county squad for summer camps. I was a left-back right through to my days in the juniors, playing at half-back now and again but certainly never seen as a forward.

I certainly never had it my head that I would go on to make a living from the game. As far as I was concerned, I would leave school and get a trade, a prospect I was perfectly happy with. As a schoolboy, I don't think I stood out from the crowd. In fact, I never even made it into the county team despite being involved in the squad. I didn't let that bother me and we were free of the pressure that surrounds youngsters in the modern game. Now, you have professional clubs scouting players in primary school and in the majority of cases these kids are being built up for a fall, considering how few make the grade. I'm a great believer in letting players of all abilities enjoy the game for as long as they can. Eventually, everyone finds their level.

From that county squad I was involved in, only Dennis Setter-ington, who went on to play for Rangers, and Danny Hood, who was picked up by the very successful Burnley side of that era, went on to play at a high level. Yet there were others who weren't involved who did make it.

Now it is probably harder than ever for people who haven't been singled out at a young age to make it because so many are written off far too early. Under Jock Wallace in the late 1970s and early 1980s, I helped with the Rangers under-16 team and I couldn't believe the vitriol being directed at those boys from parents of opposition teams on the touchline, it sickened me.

Even those who do make it into the system run the risk of being over-coached, one of the main reasons I feel there's been a real dearth of talent emerging from Scotland in recent years.

I grew up at a time when we weren't coached; we were self-taught, yet this country produced genuine world-class talent. We were free to express ourselves and find our feet without the burden of expectation, whereas I don't see our promising youngsters being given that chance to discover what it is they do best.

Rather than being coached or told what we should be doing, we relied on adults to guide us and organise football for us, and I have enormous respect for all of those who helped set me on the right path.

Tam Dalyell was one of those, long before he became an MP, when he was a teacher at Bo'ness Academy and took the county team. I always got on well with Tam and years later he invited Linda and me down to the House of Commons for lunch. It was always difficult to tell with Mr Dalyell where his allegiances really lay. I think he was a fan of football as a whole.

I left school football behind when I was 15, to begin my apprenticeship as a joiner. So much stock was placed on learning a trade and, in hindsight, I have to say that serving my time was one of the best things I ever did, because it stood me in good stead for life after football. I'm proud of my roots and certainly was never looking for a way out when full-time football came calling. I liked my work as a joiner then and I still enjoy the trade now. It has never been a chore to me and in that sense I'm lucky to have two careers in my life that I have enjoyed in very different ways.

I was a couple of years into my apprenticeship when I was asked to sign for Armadale Thistle, joining them for the 1964/65 season at a time when the club was looking to break the dominance of Linlithgow Rose. I lived with my sister Helen following my mother's death, and by that time Linda and I were an item, so I had lots of people around me willing me to do well. Linda and I married in 1969 and have just celebrated our fortieth wedding anniversary.

Training on Tuesdays and Thursdays fitted in fine with my day job, which was busy in itself since the housing industry was going through one of its boom periods in the 1960s. Armadale had a great mix of youth and experience, and I was made to feel very welcome. John Hagart, who went on to manage Hearts in the 1970s and was on the coaching staff at Ibrox during my second stint at Rangers, took the training at Thistle and there was a great atmosphere at the club. I've still got tremendous affection for Armadale, and the shirt I wore when I played for Scotland against England at Wembley in 1969 still hangs on the committee room wall at Volunteer Park as a little reminder of what they did to set me on my way.

Junior football was, and I suppose still is, a school of hard knocks. You had to grow up fast playing in that environment, and it was the making of me as a player. The fact that I always enjoyed training and the physical side of the game was a major factor in helping me hit the ground running with Armadale. I was always a fit lad, maybe down to the fact I'd played from dawn until dusk every day from the time I was knee high and wasn't afraid of putting in tough shifts on the training field. I knew that if you could get a good pre-season under your belt you already had an advantage before a ball had been kicked. It is something that applies in the juniors just as it does at the very highest level. I've encountered plenty of great players on a small pitch but when you got them out on a proper park it's a different story. Even the best in the world have to be able to cover the ground to be effective, but not everyone with talent is willing to do the dirty work in training.

My attitude and application went a long way to getting me that initial break. Armadale had always been a forward-thinking club. In fact, it was the first to host a floodlit junior game back in 1954. The club is very proud of the fact that it has sent eight Scotland internationals, and of course one England player, on the road to success over the years.

I settled quickly, playing in my usual left-back berth, but it was fairly early in my time with Thistle that I had what turned out to be a life-changing stroke of good fortune. The team arrived for a midweek game at Bo'ness without our centre forward. The appeal went out before kick-off for someone to take his place; I volunteered and marked my first ever game up front by scoring a hat-trick. It wasn't a bad start, and I never looked back.

I hadn't really thought about playing further up the park before, but I soon found I had the instinct you need to score goals. You cannot afford to dwell on the ball in the box, if you take even a single touch too many then the chance more often than not will pass. You have to be decisive and able to make snap decisions. As far as I'm concerned, it's not something you can teach; you are either a goalscorer or you're not. It just so happened that I didn't discover that I had that ability until my late teens, but once I had the chance to put it to use, the goals kept coming.

I soon found that another of the keys to success was the timing of runs and anticipation inside the box. Coupled with that, I had always been good in the air and, crucially, I was prepared to go in where the boots were flying if it meant getting on the end of a pass or a cross. Spending my formative years as a defender had helped me learn how to look out for myself and, given that the rule to outlaw tackles from behind wasn't even a twinkle in a referee's eye at that point, it proved a valuable instinct.

You had to get used to defenders going right through you, either from behind or the side, and I soon developed a reading of those situations. The thing with playing through the centre is that there is very rarely a 50–50 challenge with the ball between you and the defender. More often than not, you will receive the ball with your back to goal or have to throw yourself into challenges stacked in the defender's favour. The moment you start to fear those situations is the moment to pack in the game. I never shirked a challenge and came through my career without a serious injury, which in my mind is no coincidence.

Nobody tried to change me or the way I approached the game after my move from defence into attack, and we pushed Linlithgow Rose close on all fronts that season, ending on a high with a cup win.

The St Michael's Cup may not rank up there alongside the European Cup-Winners' Cup or the Scottish league champion-ship, but it still holds a special place in my heart. It gave me my first winner's medal, and for any player that is a big moment, whether it comes in front of 10 people on a public park or 100,000 at Hampden.

That first taste of success actually came at Easter Road, when Armadale faced Penicuik Athletic. I scored a hat-trick as we ran out 5–2 winners in front of a few thousand spectators. It was a great day for the club, who had only won the St Michael's Cup three times previously. They won it again in 2002 for the first time since that day in 1965, which brought back memories of what was obviously a very big occasion for me. It represented my last game as a junior and the start of a professional adventure that would take me all over the world and lead me into situations beyond my wildest expectations.

3

Shankly's new recruit

My cup final hat-trick at Easter Road did not go unnoticed. I was already due to travel through to Glasgow to meet with Willie Thornton, the manager of Partick Thistle, the day after the final but I never did make it to Firhill. Instead, it was Hibs who nipped in to get my signature on the first professional contract of my career. They must have known they had competition because the deal was done within a matter of minutes.

I had been aware of Partick's interest for a couple of weeks and that brought the realisation that football might soon become more than just a part-time passion for me. Thistle were in the top league at that time, the old First Division, and I very probably would have accepted their offer to join them had Hibs not beaten them to the punch.

It turned out that Bob Shankly and his trusted trainer Tom McNiven had been in the stand at Easter Road, watching from the shadows, when I hit the treble for Armadale in the St Michael's Cup final. Tom told me later that it was my running power as much as the goals that caught their eye, and they decided that they wanted to sign me.

The pair of them arrived on the doorstep of my sister Helen's house the following morning to speak to her and her husband John, who had taken me under their wing following the death of my mother and who handled that first, and arguably most important, contract of my career. Just as it was when I joined Rangers, there was no need for agents or even for negotiation.

Quite simply, I was proud to get my chance to play for Hibernian and was happy to accept whatever they offered me.

Fortunately they arrived with a very attractive proposition. In exchange for me packing in the 6 a.m. starts working as a joiner on building sites, they would replace my £3 per week wage as a tradesman with £30 per week. Armadale received the princely sum of £10, but everyone at the club was just happy to see another one of their boys earning a shot at the big time. I still remember the sense of pride I had when I went back to Armadale to present them with a ball Hibs had given me to pass on to my old club as part of the rather modest transfer package that had taken me to Leith.

The hours were a bit shorter than I was used to, with just the one training session each morning and afternoons left to ourselves. That, more than anything, took a bit of adjustment and you had to make a conscious effort not to get lazy or to fall into bad habits, given that freedom and time.

For me, that meant heading for the golf course just about every day after training. I'd never been a golfer until I turned professional in football, but I was well and truly bitten by the bug once I got started. I used to rush back from training and head straight to Linlithgow Golf Club, which was just a nine-hole course in those days. I'd go round three times a day and I loved it. In fact, the first handicap I ever had was just 10. I got as low as a handicap of 1 and represented the county in between my football commitments. A young golfer by the name of Bernard Gallacher was starting to make a name for himself at Bathgate and we became good friends. Bernie turned pro after winning the Scottish amateur title in 1967 and went on to become a real local hero, the youngest man ever to represent Great Britain and Ireland when he played in the Ryder Cup in 1969. Bernard is a Hibs fan, so there wasn't just a West Lothian link between us. Years later, he was playing down at Coventry Golf Club in Finham, while I was playing football in England, and I took my daughter Nicola along to watch him in action. She was still just a tot, so I wheeled her along to the side of the green in her buggy and told her to clap when Bernie sunk his putt she got a bit mixed up and started clapping just as he pulled the putter back. If looks could kill we would have been stone dead, then he twigged who it was. He hadn't seen us up to that point and when he realised, he cracked into the biggest grin you can imagine. It's a small world.

As well as Linlithgow, I played quite a bit at Glenbervie over the years and football opened up a few nice opportunities. Not long after going to Rangers, I remember playing in the Sean Connery pro-am down at Turnberry with the likes of Lee Trevino and Billy Casper. There was Jim Baxter and me rubbing shoulders with golf's glitterati. I'm not sure what they made of our east coast accents, but we had a whale of a time. I partnered Casper, which was an experience. He was a superstar, at the peak of his powers, and it was like watching an artist at work. On the greens in particular, he was brilliant. He was also a Mormon and days after I was pictured in the paper playing golf with him, I had a group round at the house inviting me to join their church. They obviously thought Billy had some special powers of persuasion!

I eventually had to give up golf when I started having problems with my wrist. I played with it heavily strapped, but eventually it became clear that even surgery wouldn't guarantee it could be fixed. So I packed the clubs away.

Fortunately, that was when my football days had come to an end, so throughout my career in the game I was able to stick to the routine of training in the morning and fitting in a couple of rounds in the afternoon.

It wasn't a bad life and for a young joiner from Philpstoun, it was an amazing change in fortunes. I kept my feet on the ground and knew there was a lot of hard work in front of me if I was going to make the grade. Hibs took a fresh intake of young players every year and it was survival of the fittest, physically and mentally.

The summer of 1965 was a case in point. While I was putting pen to paper on my first Hibs deal, the club was also enticing a clutch of other young players eager to make a name for themselves.

Peter Marinello, an outstanding player, was at the head of the list and there was also John Blackley, John Murphy and Colin Grant, a player I knew all about from his exploits with Linlithgow Rose.

Peter was a skelf of a boy when he arrived at Easter Road, clearly supremely talented but lethargic with it and very lightweight. I've never seen a transformation like it. After his first pre-season, he bulked up and had a new energy about him to match his talents and before long he was a household name, dubbed the new George Best by the papers. Peter left Hibs for Arsenal just one season after I moved to Rangers, costing the Gunners £100,000 as the money from the Easter Road youth policy continued to roll in, but he would be the first to admit he never fulfilled his potential.

John Blackley was a different player altogether, a rugged defender from Gairdoch Juniors who went on to become a real Hibs stalwart. John was capped by Scotland and he's still heavily involved in the game as first team coach at Plymouth Argyle, having been Paul Sturrock's trusty lieutenant for years. Colin is also still in the thick of things, heading up Aberdeen's scouting network in the north-east. He and I played quite a few games together in the early days before we went our separate ways, with Colin winding up as a player and then manager with Peterhead in the Highland League. John Murphy, a midfielder arrived from Tynecastle Athletic, had six good years with Hibs before moving on to Stirling Albion, Morton and Cowdenbeath. His career was eventually cut short by a knee injury.

We all arrived as fresh-faced rookies and to a man left Hibs as far better players for our experiences at Easter Road under Tom McNiven and Bob Shankly. Bob was not long in the door at Easter Road when he signed me at the end of the 1964/65 season. He had moved to Edinburgh at the start of 1965, having had tremendous success with Dundee which included winning the league title and taking them to within an ace of the European Cup final. He was appointed as Jock Stein's successor at Hibs and had a tall order in meeting the expectations of supporters.

The club had been genuine title challengers in that 1964/65 campaign, finishing fourth, but only four points behind the champions Kilmarnock. Just as importantly, Hibs had finished above both Rangers and Celtic. He was the right type of character to take on the task. Obviously, the Shankly family became synonymous with football and Bob's contribution sometimes gets lost in among the plaudits for his little brother Bill's achievements at Liverpool.

He could not match the success he enjoyed at Dundee with Hibs, but Bob had one arm tied behind his back. Hibs was not a wealthy club and he soon discovered the books had to be balanced by selling players. He proved himself to be adept at wheeling and dealing, but ultimately grew tired of the pretty relentless turnover of talent and left in 1969, the year after I had moved on. Many people said it was the Easter Road board's decision to sell me that proved the final straw for the manager. I don't know if that's accurate, but in truth there was very little anyone could have done to have prevented me making it to Ibrox. I would have walked over broken glass to get there.

In fairness to the manager, he did not try to influence my decision to leave Hibs. Yes, he told me he wanted me to stay and suggested I'd be better served spending at least another year as a Hibee, but there was no drama about the situation. I think he was wise enough to know when to concede defeat.

Bob Shankly was very astute and a tremendous football manager. Some may argue he was dour, but to me that was part of his charm. The Shanklys came from a similar background to myself, down-to-earth mining stock, and there was an honesty about Bob that really struck a chord with me. He knew his players well and was a good man-manager, perhaps ahead of his time in the way he handled the team. While some of his peers, including Scot Symon at Rangers, preferred to be one step removed from their squad, Bob was not afraid to get in the thick of the action in training and make his presence felt.

He also knew his football and you only have to look at the team he put out on the park at Hibs to appreciate that. His philosophy was an attacking one and even in Europe, he persisted with his five attacking players, no matter how high the stakes were. Tom McNiven was an important ally for the manager and he was a real gent. We would often moan and whine about Tom's legendary warm-ups, which seemed to go on forever, but in hindsight I can see the benefit. I can't think of a single player who suffered a hamstring strain or other muscular problem during my time training under Tom at Hibs and players from other clubs would seek him out for treatment because he was so highly respected.

We had a laugh and a joke working under Tom and Bob, but when it was time to work, it was time to work, and the players held both men in the highest regard. I came from a generation who had been taught to respect their elders and that transferred from the playground to the football field, where what the manager said was gospel.

Having been brought up on a limited ration of football, I was in my element after turning full-time in the summer of 1965 after working my notice and finishing off my joinery apprenticeship. Hibs trained on open ground at Craigentinny at that time, just down the shore from Leith and sandwiched between the docks and Portobello. We worked hard, with double sessions throughout pre-season, jogging back through the city streets to Easter Road at the end of each stint on the training field. There were regular lung-bursting runs up Arthur's Seat thrown in for good measure.

As a new player, you soon learn that the best way of endearing yourself to your new teammates is to keep your head down, work hard and try to stay out of the firing line. You have to earn respect in what can be a very intimidating environment, although we were fortunate to have some excellent experienced players who went out of their way to make the rookies feel welcome. People like Jimmy O'Rourke, Eric Stevenson and Jim Scott were major influences in the dressing room and on me personally.

Turning out in front of the big crowds never bothered me at all. I even found time to enjoy the Edinburgh derbies, despite the ferocious pace those games were played at. Hearts had a bit of an Indian sign over us during my time with Hibs, led by Donald Ford and Eddie Thomson , but it was a privilege to play in the capital derby. The games at Tynecastle were the ones I loved the most, there was something about the old ground that made it special. It always felt as though the fans were right on top of you and the pitch seemed like it had acres of space.

We may have found Hearts a tough nut to crack, but we didn't feel inferior to them on or off the park. Not long after I arrived, the new covered enclosure at Easter Road was opened, or The Shed as it was better known. There was a new set of rooms for the supporters club on Easter Road Lane and every-thing was heading in the right direction under the stewardship of the chairman William Harrower. He would pop his head round the dressing room door to wish us well before a game, but otherwise was happy to let the manager run the team.

My introduction to first-team football came earlier than I expected, after I scored 11 goals in my first dozen games for the reserves. I hadn't arrived at Easter Road with a particular game plan, but I had expected it to be a long drawn-out process to establish myself. When it all happened quickly for me, it was a very pleasant surprise.

I got the news I'd been waiting for early in 1966 on a Friday afternoon. This was it, I was going to make my Hibs debut the following day. I was excited and a little nervous, but it was what I'd been building myself up for. My first game was on 8 January against Morton at Easter Road. I didn't score, but we won 4–1 and I was happy enough with the way I played. Jimmy O'Rourke and Peter Cormack shared the goals between them but the manager must have been satisfied with what I did because I kept my place and scored my first two goals for the club at Brockville the following week against Falkirk, although it didn't prevent us from losing 3–2.

That first season was all about finding my feet and it was something similar for the team. I wasn't the only one blooded by the manager that season, with the likes of Colin Grant, Bobby Duncan and Thomson Allan also breaking through. We also had a young Pat Stanton in the side, so the future looked bright.

We finished sixth in the league that season and went into the 1966/67 campaign with confidence. On a personal level, I had a foothold in the first team and was developing a taste for football at the top level, forging a good understanding with Peter Cormack up front. Peter must have weighed six stone dripping wet, but what he lacked in bulk he more than made up for in ability. He was a great player and supplied the ammunition I thrived on, with clever little balls in behind the defenders for me to run onto. The fact that so many good players surrounded me made it simple; in many ways it was easier to play in the First Division than it was in junior football, because I was in the midst of so much talent. Pat Stanton was another who could see a pass in an instant and knew exactly where I wanted the ball, and I was in my element in that sort of company, both on and off the park.

I travelled through from West Lothian to Edinburgh every day by train, joining Jim Scott and John Blackley as well as a player called Bobby Hogg for the journey. Bobby later emigrated to Australia, but at that time we were all very close and built up a cracking camaraderie on the trips to and from work each day.

The only change was on match days, when we'd alter our route and head straight for the Dundas Hotel in the centre of Edinburgh for a light pre-match meal before being taken by bus or car to the ground.

It wasn't until I passed my driving test as a 19-year-old that the daily routine of getting the train to work was broken, taking the car a couple of days a week. Not long after I earned my licence, my future brother-in-law Bill helped me get my hands on my first car. Bill, a policeman, found me a gleaming dark blue Vauxhall through a garage in Edinburgh, and I was proud as punch as I drove into the ground for the first time. There were no Bentleys or BMWs filling the car parks of football grounds in those days, we relied on more modest means to get us from A to B. My little motor was dwarfed sitting next to the manager's big green Ford Zephyr. But I didn't care, I loved it.

The trappings of success were one thing, but what happened on the pitch mattered most and that 1967/68 season was one to remember for Hibs. We went into European competition, taking part in the Fairs Cup. After beating Racing Club of Paris in the first round, we were drawn against Napoli and it turned out to be a cracker of a tie. In the first leg we lost 4–1 in Naples and everyone wrote us off. Everyone except Mr Shankly that is, he remained confident that we could make it through and told the press as much before the game. And he was right.

That game in Italy was a real eye opener for me. It was one of my earliest experiences of playing abroad, and southern Italy was not a bad place to learn the ropes. The old saying, See Naples and Die, was very appropriate because the atmosphere inside the Stadio San Paolo wasn't for the faint-hearted. Harrowing is the best way to describe it. The ground had been built just a few years previously and the crowd was right on top of you. It was bedlam. I scored our only goal at their place as Jose Altafini ran us ragged. Fortunately, the Brazilian was injured for the second leg; one less problem to worry about against a team packed with top-class players. Altafini had made his name with AC Milan, but even in the latter stages of his career with Napoli he was still a class act, a natural footballer who looked capable of opening us up every time he got hold of the ball. Playing against opponents of that calibre can only make you a better player and I loved every minute of that European campaign with Hibs, not least the return leg against the Italians.

At Easter Road, we produced a storming display to win 5–0 against the men from Naples. Their intention was to out-muscle us but we were a match physically and mentally. It was my first real experience of the way the continental teams tried to grind down opponents, but I had the last laugh, scoring the fifth to win the tie 6–4 on aggregate.

Bobby Duncan, Pat Quinn and Peter Cormack put us on the comeback trail before Pat Stanton made it 4–0 on the night and 5–5 on aggregate. Napoli shipped the same number of goals against us that night as they had in their previous six matches, so they were no pushovers. Dino Zoff, who was in goal for them that night, looked shell-shocked as we picked them apart. Whilst Altafini was on his way down, Zoff was very much heading in the opposite direction. By the end of that season, he was Italy's first-choice goalkeeper and had a European Championship winner's medal in his pocket. Zoff, who won the World Cup in 1982, was a rising star in Italian football and despite his lack of height he had amazing reflexes. That day he didn't have an answer to us though.

It was the best performance of my time at Hibs and a pleasure to be involved in. The atmosphere at Easter Road that night was like nothing I had experienced. It whetted my appetite for the really big European nights and gave me the belief that I could

mix it with the most accomplished in the business. Italy were
Europe's best national side and the club teams were no slouches
either. The season we played Napoli, they were nip and tuck
with Milan right the way through the season, eventually finishing runners-up.

For us to dump them out of the competition showed we had
potential and that was put to the test in the next round of the
Fairs Cup, when we played Don Revie's legendary Leeds United
team. The first leg was down at Elland Road, where we lost 1–0
and I found out all about the physical threat that Leeds side
posed. Billy Bremner, whom I later played alongside for Scotland, cut me down to size very early in proceedings and I was
stretchered off with ligament damage. Billy later said he would
never have done that if he had got to know me sooner, but it
wasn't a great consolation. When Billy hit you with one of his
tackles, you knew all about it and I needed four weeks to recover
from my brief encounter with him. I never held a grudge
though, as far as I was concerned I always gave as good as I got.

Mind you, it wasn't just Bremner that you had to worry about
when you were up against Leeds. I'll never forget Revie's assistant
patrolling the touchline snarling at his players and egging them on
as they hunted us down. It was a fierce tie. Norman Hunter and
Johnny Giles could look after themselves too, but there was silk to
go with their steel through the likes of Eddie Gray. It was Jack
Charlton's goal at Elland Road that separated the sides in the end,
but we weren't off the pace and showed what we were capable of
with a 1–1 draw in the return leg. I actually scored against Leeds,
kneeing the ball out of their goalkeeper Gary Sprake's hands and
into the net, but the linesman flagged to disallow it after the
referee had signalled a goal. It wasn't to be, unfortunately, and we
went back to league business on our way to finishing third in the
First Division.

European football brought some amazing experiences, but
that extended beyond competition. Football gave me so many

opportunities at a very young age, not least the chance to see the world. I very nearly missed out on a tour of North America when I broke out in chicken pox just before the team left Scotland. I was all kitted out with my suit and desperate to leave when I took ill and it required some persuading before I was finally allowed to fly out a couple of weeks later to join the rest of the squad. We took part in a tournament playing as Toronto, with several other British teams representing other American and Canadian cities. Aberdeen were there, playing as the Washington Whips, and it was a well-run tour. We darted here, there and everywhere, taking in Dallas and Chicago as well as Vancouver and Houston.

There was also a pre-season tour of Africa in 1968, playing a series of games in Nigeria and Ghana, and those trips made you grow up pretty quickly. The African adventure in the summer of 1968 proved to be my final pre-season as an Easter Road player, but there was plenty of drama in the final few months of my time in Leith.

Before I left for Ibrox, there was a League Cup run that took Hibs all the way to the final at Hampden which brought its own joy and pain for me. The competition was played on a sectional basis and we didn't get off to the best of starts, losing to St Johnstone in a game that saw Peter Cormack badly injured. We bounced back by beating Raith Rovers and then Falkirk. I scored against the Bairns and hit another couple in the return fixture against St Johnstone, a 2–2 draw, before we hammered Raith 3–0 and beat Falkirk 2–0 to qualify for the knock-out stage of the competition.

We defeated East Fife 6–2 over two legs in the quarter-finals and I grabbed a goal in each of those games, as well as another in the semi-final against Dundee at Tynecastle, a game we won 2–1 thanks to Allan McGraw's winner. Even then, Allan had his knees heavily bandaged, an early sign of the injuries which plagued him later in life. It pains me to see the agony Allan has to endure with his knees, needing help to get upstairs because of the effects of painkilling injections he received for years on end to keep him soldiering on, but it will never take away the great memories of him during his playing days.

Thanks to Allan, we were through to Hampden to face Celtic in the final and my first shot at a winner's medal was in sight. The manager took us away to Berwick to make sure there were no distractions for the build-up to the final, aside from a brief leave of absence for a Clancy Brothers concert back at the Playhouse, and we were well prepared. Then, with the big match looming, word began to break that there had been a fire at Hampden. It was nothing major but it was enough to persuade the league to postpone the final and with that decision I was robbed of the chance of a dream send-off.

By the time the rearranged game was played, at the tail-end of the season rather than the traditional winter slot, I was a Rangers player and I ended up at the back of the Hampden stand watching my old teammates being roundly beaten by Celtic. They lost 6–2 and it was a strange one for me, having played my part in getting Hibs to the final but being totally removed from it.

I didn't leave with a medal, but walked out the door with my head held high and proud to have served the club I'd grown up watching. I never gave less than my all in a Hibs shirt, but it was time to move onwards and upwards. Ibrox was calling.

4

The £100,000 player

At Easter Road, I was one of many fish in the big pond of the capital city. Overnight, I became a very big fish in the goldfish bowl of Old Firm football and it was something I quickly had to learn to deal with. In some ways, the game becomes a side issue when you join either one of Glasgow's big two and I wasn't even through the door at Ibrox before I discovered that first-hand.

On the morning of my first training session with my new Ibrox teammates, my name was splashed across every newspaper in the country. I had been growing used to more media interest as I established myself at Hibs, but nothing could have prepared me for the intensity of the coverage of my transfer to Rangers.

It was big news and the size of the fee was making the biggest headlines. The £100,000 transfer shattered the Rangers club record, which had remained at £65,000 since Alex Ferguson had arrived in 1967, and was by far and away the biggest deal brokered between Scottish clubs. It appeared that for every pound Rangers had spent, there was a column inch of copy about the move and it put everything into sharp focus for me.

I had been used to a quiet life at Easter Road, free to go about my work without distraction. Yes, I had been well-known in football circles, but when you play for an Old Firm side you find the lines become blurred. Every player becomes a household name, and nothing can prepare you for that.

Even before I'd kicked a ball for Rangers, I realised that life at Ibrox would be different. The encouraging thing from my perspective was that nobody in the media was questioning the wisdom of spending so big, but at the same time I knew I would be judged quickly. I would have to start repaying that £100,000 pretty soon.

Learning to deal with my new place as Scotland's big-money man was all part of the transition for me.

To me it was unimportant, but to the press and the football public it appeared to matter a great deal. At every ground I went to, supporters were quick to remind me of the price tag around my neck, not least if things weren't going to plan.

The fans I could live with, they pay their money and can say what they like, but I found the approach from opposition players more puzzling. I can honestly say that in a decade and a half as a professional football player with Hibs, Rangers and Coventry City, I never once worried about the player I was up against. Whether it was Bayern Munich or Brechin City, reputations did not matter one bit to me. I soon found out that not everyone approached the game in the same spirit.

With the ink barely dry on the cheque, opposition defenders began chirping away during games about the fee. To me, it was an odd tactic. It wasn't something I was ashamed of, if I was worth 10 times what they were it didn't reflect badly on me as far as I could see. I found myself being marked tighter than I ever had been before and I had to come to terms with the attention I was receiving. Other big-money signings hadn't fulfilled their potential with Rangers, people like Alex Smith and even Alex Ferguson to a certain extent, and if I wanted to avoid doing the same, I couldn't afford to dwell on the price tag I had been labelled with.

On and off the park, it felt as though I was up on a pedestal, or maybe a parapet. There were certainly plenty of people gunning for me, but I was ready to meet them head on.

The flip side of that coin is that there were also hundreds of thousands of people right behind me. When you join Rangers, you inherit more than just a new employer's name on your wage packet; you gain the backing of a truly phenomenal group of supporters.

Between the car park and the front door at Ibrox, I've seen it take half an hour to get through the autograph hunters and well-wishers. For a bashful boy from the country, this was a new experience, but it brought home the size of the club and the strength of feeling surrounding Rangers. I remember when I left Hibs speaking to Alex Scott, who had played for both Rangers and Everton, about the path I had chosen. He loved his time at Everton but told me I'd made the right decision, that I was going to the best club in the business. Not long after arriving at Ibrox, I began to realise exactly what he meant and not once did I ever regret my decision. If Everton hadn't pressed me quite so hard for a decision, there's a chance I might have talked myself into the move to Goodison, but if I had done that I would have missed out on the most magical period in my career, the Ibrox years.

The adulation heaped upon Rangers players was on a whole new level to anything I'd seen at Hibs, just as the passion with which we were disliked by Celtic supporters was far more intense than the rivalry between the two Edinburgh clubs. Depending on which side of the divide they were from, the greeting from people in the street was very different and it made the daily walk through Glasgow city centre interesting, to say the least.

Both of those things combined, the love and the hatred, were factors in my decision not to relocate to the west coast after signing for Rangers. The club was pretty insistent that I should move to the Glasgow area and had searched out houses in Newton Mearns for me. Ronnie McKinnon and a clutch of fellow Rangers players already lived in that area of the city. It was the up-and-coming suburb at the time, with a lot of new houses. I've no doubt it would have been a lovely place to live and, sitting on the south side of town, it was very handily placed for Ibrox, but there was a nagging doubt in my mind. I couldn't convince myself that moving to Glasgow wouldn't bring me more attention than I was already attracting, and I made my mind up pretty quickly that it wouldn't be right for us.

The issue of where I would live hadn't even cropped up during negotiations over the move. Both Rangers and I were so wrapped up in completing the deal that the finer details never even became part of the discussion, which was all about football rather than logistics.

While I understood why Davie White was keen for me to cut out the cross-country trek each day, I felt there was a danger of being suffocated if I became wrapped up in Glasgow life. I love the city, love the people and the football supporters, but you need an escape from the pressure cooker of the Old Firm and for me that lay at home in West Lothian.

While the manager had urged me to move, he accepted my decision to stay put in Philpstoun. At that time, there was a strong east coast contingent who travelled through by train each day and I joined a group led by John Greig and Sandy Jardine from Edinburgh and which also included Willie Johnston and Willie Mathieson from Fife as well as Billy McPhee. We'd roll into Queen Street each morning and hitch a lift in taxis through to Ibrox to get ready for training, a ritual that was never detrimental in my opinion. In many ways, the time we spent travelling helped to bring us closer together and the journeys flew by. John Greig eventually moved through to Glasgow when he took over as manager, but he spent his entire playing career commuting from east to west. For me it was ideal.

Once Rangers had accepted that I wasn't willing to move to Glasgow, I struck a deal to secure my first house just a hop and skip from my home village. I was only six weeks into my contract when the chairman, John Lawrence, agreed to buy it for me. I'd made a good start to my career at Ibrox and struck while the iron was hot.

Mr Lawrence provided me with a new family home in Linlithgow, with the club footing the £6,000 bill. When you consider property prices today, I wish I'd bought a whole street, but I was delighted with my first step onto the housing ladder. It was a generous gesture by the club, but I like to think I repaid them with my performances over the years that followed.

Looking back at that particular part of the transfer deal, it provides an indication of just how vast the investment was by Rangers in a player as young as I was when they signed me. Never mind buying a whole street of houses, Rangers could have had themselves a whole estate of hundreds of houses for the money they shelled out on me. In today's money, it would have been a multi-million pound deal and it was not the norm for the directors to sanction that level of spending.

It took Rangers the best part of a decade to sign another six-figure cheque, with Davie Cooper arriving from Clydebank in 1977, and it wasn't really until the 1980s that those types of figures became commonplace in Scotland.

It was a big deal and the resultant media scrum was understandable, but at the time it really didn't weigh on my mind. Perhaps if I had moved to Glasgow and lived in the Old Firm spotlight I may have felt greater pressure. I certainly never allowed my feet to leave the ground and being able to go back to my home patch, where everyone knew me as a person and not as a star, was a massive part of that.

I was surrounded by the people I grew up with, who knew me best, and if they'd felt I was getting too big for my boots I would soon have heard about it.

I was able to go for a night out in Linlithgow without being bothered by a soul. In Glasgow, that would have been impossible and our existence would have been very different.

The new house apart, my lifestyle didn't change dramatically after moving to Rangers. We did treat ourselves to a nice honeymoon when we married in 1969, booking ourselves into the Delfin Playa Hotel in the centre of Palma Nova on Majorca. It was Davie White who recommended it to us and we loved it from the minute we stepped through the front door. When we were shown to our room, there were flowers and champagne waiting for us, signed by Davie. It was a lovely touch. Then when we went down for breakfast the next day, Linda said, 'You'll never guess who just walked in – it's your manager.' I liked Davie, but I hadn't bargained on spending my honeymoon with him! It turned out that he had been due to spend his summer holiday at a villa nearby but hadn't liked it and decided to check into the Delfin.

He wasn't the only familiar face mind you, with Celtic's Bertie Auld and Willie Wallace in the same hotel and my Ibrox teammate Bobby Watson there, too. Maybe not surprisingly, we got roped into a bounce game against the Spanish waiters, with Davie White taking on the role of player-manager. The head waiter was a fierce little character who was always bawling at his staff. He also fancied himself as a right winger, so I put myself at left back and gave him an absolute mauling. His colleagues certainly liked seeing him being dumped on his backside, the service Linda and I received for the rest of the stay was amazing! We had a great time, even borrowing Davie's hire car to tour round the island, and with the wedding behind us it was the first time we really had a chance to sit back and enjoy our new life.

Back home, there was no real change to the day-to-day routine, except for the fact that the train I caught to work each day went west instead of east. The clothes I wore did change, though.

At Hibs, there was no dress code; at Ibrox there was a strict policy, a legacy from the great Bill Struth's days. Everyone was expected to wear a collar and tie and there were no exceptions to the rule. I had to rush out and get measured for new shirts and suits after signing, and it certainly took a bit of getting used to, having to regularly dress up in what previously would have been my Sunday best. Never mind the keys to a house, my earliest perks at Ibrox were a couple of club ties. I've still got them, there was something special about getting my hands on them.

The dress code was fairly unique to Ibrox, but it's something that many players carried with them. Willie Johnston tells the story about turning up at Hearts, after leaving Rangers, in a collar and tie and being greeted by bemused looks. But once you had lived the Rangers way, paying attention to every detail, no matter how big or small, it was difficult to shake the good habits that had been instilled in you. Maybe that's why so many players get disillusioned, after leaving Ibrox any other club is second best.

Having settled into my life as a Ranger, I soon found that the opportunities did not stop just because my future was settled. Not long after I arrived, Dan Patrick invited me to appoint him as my agent. It wasn't something I had seriously contemplated, because they just weren't part of the game in the 1960s. I can't recall any other Rangers player who had agents representing them, but Dan was a persuasive character who promised he would top up my income, minus his cut of the profits, of course. In fact, he promised we would make a lot of money together.

Dan, who was based in Bishopbriggs, became my publicist as well as my agent. He set up a series of exclusive interviews with the *Daily Express*, something I'm sure the other papers frowned upon, and also negotiated a string of public appearances.

I was roped into opening garages and shops, but I really didn't find any of those types of events a chore. They always attracted plenty of Rangers supporters and we had good fun.

Even with my new agent in tow, I ensured football came first. No matter how much I had cost the club, how much I was earning or what offers I had on the table, there was no thrill to beat scoring goals for Rangers.

5

Living the dream

A player's debut can set the tone for the rest of his career with a club. Get off to a good start and you're a hero, but if you stumble your way through that first match, then straight away you find yourself in trouble. Either way, there's usually no going back.

I don't know any individual who doesn't suffer pre-match nerves, although nervousness in itself is maybe a misleading term. What you feel is excitement combined with anticipation that brings a special energy, and when it comes to your first game for any team that feeling is much more intense. The fact that I may as well have had a big price tag hanging around my neck when the curtain went up on my life as a Rangers player only served to enhance the buzz surrounding the occasion, not just for me but for the fans, too.

My first game fell on 2 November 1968. It was a dark and moody Saturday afternoon in conditions typical of a Scottish winter, and the surroundings were as far removed from the glamour and prestige of Ibrox as you could possibly encounter in the First Division.

Gayfield Park in Arbroath was the setting and, as anyone who has ever been to that fine little ground will testify, it is as earthy a place as you'll find in the Scottish game. There was a biting chill in the air as that familiar east coast wind whipped in off the North Sea just beyond the club's back wall. It has to be the coldest place to play football in the country, but it holds many memories for me. The fact that the old place hasn't changed much over the years has helped to preserve them.

I had signed just days before, but I was confident I would feature at Arbroath. When Davie White announced the team on the Friday, the news I was waiting for was broken to me. Colin Stein No. 9. In the previous game, Rangers had beaten Dundalk 6–1 in a Fairs Cup tie, with Alex Ferguson and Willie Henderson both scoring doubles to add to a John Greig effort and an own goal by the luckless Irishmen.

Despite that emphatic midweek result, the manager wasn't afraid to make changes. Fergie, even after his two goals, was dropped to the bench. He may not have liked it at the time, but I wonder now with all of his experience on the other side of the desk if he can appreciate the position Davie White found himself in.

Fergie had been the club's record signing until my arrival, but he obviously was not untouchable. That wasn't lost on me, and I knew my own place as the most expensive player on the books wouldn't bring any guarantees if I didn't set the heather on fire.

The team lines from that day still trip off the tongue: Norrie Martin, Kai Johansen, Willie Mathieson, John Greig, Ronnie McKinnon, Dave Smith, Willie Henderson, Andy Penman, Colin Stein, Willie Johnston and Orjan Persson.

Every one of my 10 teammates that day, or 11 if you include Fergie's introduction from the bench, possessed undoubted ability. I performed alongside some supremely gifted players at Easter Road, but I remember looking around the pitch as I warmed up for my Rangers debut and thinking that if I couldn't play in this type of company, with such great men around me, I shouldn't be in the game. There was strength and steel, craft and guile, and a pace to the way the team played that you did not appreciate looking in from the outside. As a forward, you rely so much on those around you and I could tell within minutes of setting foot on the park with my new colleagues that life was about to get a whole lot better, because the service they provided was wonderful.

Mind you, it wasn't just those who were on the pitch that took my breath away. The supporters who flocked to Gayfield made it a day to remember. Almost 10,000 people crammed inside the compact little stadium that day, with barely any room for those on the terraces to move. There must have been 60 Arbroath fans, because all I could see were Rangers colours sprawling all round the pitch. The drive up to the ground was astonishing, I'd never seen so much red, white and blue, the streets were mobbed. We travelled through by coach from Glasgow and the further along the road we travelled, the stronger grew the realisation that I was about to become a Rangers player. I wish we could have stepped off the bus straight onto the pitch, but instead it was a case of killing time. I've watched teammates go through the oddest rituals and adhere to the same superstitions before every game, but I never bought into any of that, instead I was dressed and ready to go, with plenty of time to spare and champing at the bit. Pulling on the light blue jersey for the first time sent a tingle down my spine. I'd waited all my life to do it and now it was my time to shine.

I had to do a double-take when the travelling support started chanting my name. It wasn't so long ago that the same fans had been calling me for everything when I'd been in green and white, but now they were firmly in my corner. It meant the world to me to have that type of acceptance before I'd even kicked a ball. It also brought home to me that everyone at Gayfield that day would have their eyes planted in my direction; it would soon be time to stand and deliver.

The hour leading up to a game is always the most difficult to fill, but that day it felt like an eternity. You do your limbering up, but your mind is already racing and all that matters is hearing that first whistle and getting the ball rolling. On this occasion, I was even more eager than usual and when the match eventually started, it was brilliant, everything I'd worked so hard for was just about to come to fruition. I was now a Rangers player.

There was an awful lot of pressure on Davie White going into the game. He'd spent a lot of money to sign me and his wisdom was about to be tested in full public view. He never let on how much he needed a big performance from me, instead he had a quiet word in my ear and told me to do my best.

I spent the first half finding my feet. I was playing in a new team with different characters and different styles. Even the pace of the passing was up a notch from what I was used to at Hibs and as a striker you need to build up an understanding with those who are trusted to supply the ammunition. Bob Shankly had employed an attacking philosophy in Leith and at Rangers I was delighted to find the same attitude. Every player had licence to get forward and there was a wonderful mix, from the resolve of Greig and McKinnon to the subtlety of Smith and Persson and unpredictability of Johnston and Henderson.

I had to carve out my own niche and didn't intend to waste any time, even if I did need a bit of breathing space to adjust. I'm the first to admit that my first 45 minutes of football for Rangers were hardly dynamite. I had as quiet a half as I can ever remember and it was pretty clear that Arbroath had set out to try to spoil my particular party. I became used to being closely patrolled after joining Rangers and that first day was no different, defenders were breathing down my neck at every turn.

Fortunately, we were far from a one-man team and my new strike partner was taking care of business. Mark Hateley and Alistair McCoist took months to establish their partnership together at Rangers, but fortunately for Willie Johnston and me the chemistry came far quicker. He was a joy to play alongside, although his versatility ensured he wasn't restricted to playing through the centre and I had my share of strike partners at Ibrox.

Bud, who had that streak of devilment to go along with his other qualities, tucked away two goals in the first half at Arbroath to establish what looked like a comfortable lead. When the home team pulled one back just after the break, you could sense the tension beginning to build in the stand and three enclosures that circled the park, all bursting at the seams with Rangers supporters.

It wasn't just the vocal backing that gave the match its atmosphere; the supporters had a little extra something up their sleeves. The game was just a few days before Bonfire Night and there were fireworks being set off on the terraces, so every now and again there would be a flurry of what sounded like shots ringing out around the ground. It may have been winter, but the atmosphere was sensational and the whole feeling set the stage for a great game.

Arbroath had just come up from the old Second Division and were still trying to establish themselves in the top flight. They must have wished they had never won promotion that day because once we got into our stride they just didn't have an answer. Orjan Persson and Willie Henderson tortured them down the wings and as a striker it was there on a plate for me to make an impact.

With the game hanging in the balance at 2–1, I came up with a pretty dramatic way to end any lingering doubts, banging in a hat-trick in double-quick time to put us out of sight of Arbroath. Some reports say the goals came inside four minutes, others put it at six minutes. Whatever the figure was, I can still remember the feeling of pure elation as they flew into the net. The noise was deafening and the fans were going wild. They may have been chanting my name before kick-off but now that I'd given them something to really shout about, they sounded twice as loud.

I always went out with the belief that I would score, but never made predictions about hat-tricks. One goal would have done me fine to mark my debut, to score three was just out of this world and it gave me a story to tell when I went home to be greeted by Linda, who had been too nervous to come and watch on the day. I understood, because I know from watching my brothers play that it's far easier when you're out on the pitch, and able to make a difference, than when you're stranded on the touchlines. My sisters were in the crowd though, caught up in the whole occasion, and it was a game to cherish.

Persson, the classy Swedish winger, set me up for the first one and for the next few minutes everything I hit made it into the net. It was a phenomenal period of play and arguably one of the most important spells in my career. With those goals, I gained the instant approval of the Rangers supporters and with that in your hip pocket you can't go wrong.

A hat-trick on your first game is not a bad way to win friends and influence people, although it is something of a rarity at Rangers. Alex Scott had scored three on his debut in the 1950s, no mean achievement for a winger, and I was next in line. It took near enough four decades for Kris Boyd to become the next when he walked away with the match ball after his debut against Peterhead in a cup tie in 2006.

While I was delighted with this flying start, you can imagine how much it meant to Davie White. He'd had enough faith in me to spend a small fortune on my transfer fee and you could see the joy and relief on his face at full-time. He was waiting with a pat on the back for me at the end. In one fell swoop, the decision to buy me as well as catapult me straight into the team had been vindicated.

I was relieved to come through a tough work-out. I was up against a defender called Ian Stirling that day and he gave me a pretty tough examination. He was hard but fair, not getting caught up in the hype surrounding my transfer and treating it like any other game. If every team had treated it that way, it would have been far better, instead of getting wrapped up in the size of the fee and trying to put me in my place. Because I found myself being man-marked in practically every match after moving to Rangers, I had to learn to become more mobile, to continually keep on my toes and move across the forward line. Davie White encouraged all of the attacking players to switch as often as possible during a game anyway, so it fitted with what he wanted from us as a team, trying to stay one step ahead of the opposition.

Arbroath gave us a good game but we came out of it well. There wasn't too much time for congratulations though, because it was straight back to work as we prepared for our home match against Hibs a week later. Obviously it was going to be a massive afternoon for me, and it didn't disappoint.

After my hurried exit from Easter Road, it was the first real chance I had to meet up with my old teammates and there were a few words exchanged before, during and after the game. It was all good-natured stuff, with Jimmy O'Rourke, as always, leading the wind-ups. Jimmy was the joker in the Hibs pack and Pat Stanton was the dour one, they were like a comedy double act.

For home games, we always did our warm-up in the big tunnel area, where there was room for a kick-about, and there was plenty of banter flying around that day. I had left behind some great friends at Hibs, not least in the shape of goalkeeper Thomson Allan. Thomson went on to be best man at my wedding but he was a bit more complimentary in that role than he was on the day we went head-to-head on the pitch.

Thomson had come in for Willie Wilson, but he ended up wishing he hadn't. We were red hot that day and my hat-trick helped us on our way to a 6–1 victory against a team who had championship aspirations. Hibs simply didn't lose by that type of margin, but on the day they had no answer to us.

Joe McBride, who had been signed from Celtic to fill my place at Easter Road, could do nothing to turn the tide and it ended up a one-sided contest. I didn't tire of telling Thomson later in the evening, when we were out for a quiet drink, about our fine form, although he had already seen it at first-hand. One of the other goals that day was a screamer from Orjan Persson, so the goals were flying in from all departments. I bought Thomson a few drinks to numb the pain and it did nothing to harm our friendship, which had built up from our days with the county squad as schoolboys.

In the weeks before I left Hibs, there were sections of the Easter Road crowd who started jeering me, obviously not happy with the prospect of me leaving. They pay their money and are entitled to their opinions but I would challenge any football supporter to put their hand on their heart and say they would turn down the opportunity to better themselves professionally and financially. Logic went out of the window and because I dared to look for bigger and better things, I was singled out. That made the three goals against Hibs even sweeter.

It was a new experience for me to be playing in front of such a home crowd and I can tell you it is far easier playing with 60,000 supporters cheering for you than it is when they are giving you pelters. If the atmosphere was good at Arbroath, inside Ibrox it was phenomenal.

What I was already beginning to appreciate was the appetite for success at Rangers. The supporters don't just hope for victory, they expect it. It doesn't matter if it is Arbroath or AC Milan you are playing, the demands are just the same. There have been plenty of stark reminders of that in Rangers' history and I benefited from the rather harsh zero-tolerance approach to failure. It takes a certain type of mentality to cope with that pressure and not everyone is cut out for it. The players who last the longest and play the most games are those with the strength of character, maybe even bloody-mindedness, to keep trying no matter what is thrown at you. Others get lost along the way.

Four days after that fantastic performance against Hibs, we faced Dundalk over in Ireland in the second leg of the Fairs Cup second round. After the 6–1 win at Ibrox, achieved just before I signed, the result was never in doubt so the game should have been a total non-event.

My trebles in the previous two fixtures changed that though. It felt like the whole country was obsessed with whether or not I could make it a hat-trick of hat-tricks.

The papers were full of it and the bookmakers were taking advantage of the interest that was being stoked up. Mind you, the odds were far from generous. John Smith, the big-name bookie on the west coast at that time, was quoting me at just 6–4 to score three against the men from the Emerald Isle. Given three consecutive hat-tricks are pretty much unheard-of, it felt a bit harsh. I certainly wasn't tempted to put a few quid on myself given those odds, surely at least 10–1 would have been fair!

The serious side of it was that people were also able to bet against me scoring another hat-trick, and having floods of money being waged on my performance actually had an impact on me. Whatever happened, I knew it was going to cost a lot of people a lot of money and for the first time I felt like a pawn in a game I had no control of. The manager and the rest of the team knew I was upset by it and tried to lighten the mood with a laugh and a joke, but it was still there at the back of my mind.

Dundalk's place was similar to Gayfield, compact but close to bursting point. Their team may have been dead and buried, but the Irish supporters were never going to stay away from this one.

Alex Ferguson came back into the side, with Davie White putting out a strong team despite the lead from the first leg, but there was another notable face that night. A young Alfie Conn, coming on from the bench, made his Rangers debut and even that early it was clear that he had what it took to play at the top level.

By the time Alfie was introduced, I was on track to prove the bookmakers were right to have me at short odds for another hat-trick. I sank two to set myself up to keep the run going and was within a hair's breadth of getting the third all of the punters were banking on. With five minutes to go I crashed a shot off the post and the ball rolled agonisingly across the line to safety. I thought, just like everyone else in the ground, that it was going in, but it would have been churlish to complain about only scoring the eight goals in my first three games. If I'd been offered that sort of return when I joined, I would have happily accepted.

Willie Mathieson made it 3–0 to secure a 9–1 win on aggregate and both at home and in Europe, everything looked rosy in the garden.

Football has a funny habit of bringing you back down to earth, though, and predictably that's exactly what happened to both me and the team when we returned to home soil on the back of the Fairs Cup win.

Three days after hammering Dundalk, we made the short hop to Paisley to play St Mirren in the league and we had a nightmare, losing 1–0 in a game we should have won by a country mile. Sometimes in games nothing goes for you and this was one of those occasions. We had a succession of chances and the ball landed everywhere but in the back of the net. Denis Connaghan played in goal for the Buddies that afternoon and he haunted us. I thought I'd beaten him when I got on the end of an Andy Penman cross and Denis dived the wrong way but, typical of that day, my effort hit his toe and the ball trundled away from the goal.

Losing a football match is never nice. I hated it. Losing a football match when you know hundreds of thousands of people are hanging on the result makes it so much worse. Every game you play for the Rangers comes with that added pressure, winning is not what the supporters hope for, it is what they demand.

At Love Street, I had never seen anything like it. There were more than 40,000 inside the ground and, just as it had been in Arbroath, it was a sea of red, white and blue all around the ground. Not giving them the result they wanted was hard to bear and we stuttered for a couple of weeks after that, drawing against Clyde and Airdrie. I scored in both of those fixtures, and again in the next game when we beat my brother's Raith Rovers side 3–0 in Kirkcaldy.

That signalled the start of a run of five wins and put our championship challenge back on track. The sequence of victories culminated in my first Old Firm experience. What a day that was. Trying to describe what it feels like to play in the world's greatest derby match is a tall order. Even as a professional player, an international by that stage, nothing could have prepared me for it. The whole week building up to an Old Firm encounter is manic, there's just no escape from it. All anyone wants to talk about is the match. We'd already beaten Celtic 4–2 early in the season, before my arrival, and everyone was acutely aware that doing the double would give us a real psychological edge in the second half of the campaign.

Running out in front of 85,000 people at Ibrox was breathtaking. You come out of the tunnel to be met by a wall of noise like nothing else in the world and you can feel the passion spilling over from the terraces. It's an instant adrenalin rush and once you have tasted that occasion, everything else seems tame in comparison.

My Old Firm debut went well, we won 1–0 through a John Greig penalty, and we were on the charge. After beating Celtic, we drew at Kilmarnock but then won our next six games in the First Division. We were also going well in Europe and everything looked rosy. It should have been the best of times, but for me nothing ran smoothly. One of the biggest nightmares of my entire career was waiting just round the corner.

6

Controversy, conspiracy and cup heartache

It is one thing playing in the Glasgow derby but quite another to find yourself at the centre of an Old Firm conspiracy theory. That's the unenviable position I found myself in just months after landing on the doorstep at Ibrox. After a flying start to my life as a Rangers player, the wheels came tumbling off in the most spectacular and controversial circumstances. Just like everything in my life at that time, it happened in full public view and everyone had their opinion on what unfolded.

The drama began in familiar surroundings on the park at Ibrox and very nearly ended up in a court room. For the first time, I found myself at loggerheads with the power-brokers at Rangers and learnt a very valuable lesson: no man is bigger than the club.

It all kicked off in a home game against Clyde. It was a league match and the date, 15 March 1969, is ingrained in my mind. After a lean spell in scoring terms, I'd come back into form with a bang and hammered a hat-trick past a Bully Wee side that was fighting for survival. We were cruising to a 6–0 win with just minutes to play, still sitting pretty to push for the championship, closing in on Celtic, when I collected the ball deep in the Clyde half and set off on a run across the pitch. Eddie Mulheron, the opposition left back, tracked me all the way and started taking pot shots, swinging wildly with his boot and making no attempt to play the ball.

He must have kicked me five or six times before I finally snapped, the red mist came down and I retaliated. If the referee had given a free-kick when Mulheron first tried to scythe me down it would never have happened; instead I ended up taking matters into my own hands. After being kicked at for fully 40-yards, I'd had enough.

I turned on my opposite number and kicked him right back. Unfortunately, I had done enough to merit a red card, something I couldn't argue with since I had landed a few blows.

Ian Foote was the referee and as he sent me packing, he actually told me that he would have sent Mulheron off for what he'd done to me if I'd given him the chance. That wasn't much consolation and it was no defence on his part. If Foote had done his job and stopped the game when the assault on me began, he would have had the perfect chance to get his cards out and deal with the main offender. I was practically dragged of the park by Alex Ferguson and our trainer Davie Kinnear, absolutely beside myself after what had happened. Fergie was trying to tell me that I would only make things worse for myself by trying to argue with the referee, but it was going in one ear and out the other, I was absolutely devastated,

Mulheron was the one who instigated it all, but it was me who bore the brunt. I know I shouldn't have risen to the bait but I was never the most patient of men on the football pitch and I was pushed past my limit. He was sent off for his part in the clash, but he should have been red-carded long before then.

The game was won and two more vital league points were in the bag. There were just two minutes left, so the sensible thing would have been just to walk away and keep my distance from Mulheron, who appeared intent on putting me out of the game, but I'd never shirked a challenge and wasn't about to start.

I wouldn't recognise Eddie Mulheron if he walked through my front door, to be honest. There had been no bad blood between us before that game as far as I can recall and I don't even remember any previous run-ins, although he had been at Clyde for as long as I'd been a professional so we must have played against each other in the years leading up to that incident. All I do know is on that day he was hell-bent on bringing me down. The last I heard, he was in South Africa, so there's a lot more distance between us now than there was that day when he was trying to break my legs. Many years later, I played in a golf pro-am with a man who turned out to be his cousin. Not surprisingly, he kept quiet about his family connection all the way round, until he blurted out at the end who his cousin was. I told him to tell Eddie that I hadn't been asking for him.

As a striker, you have to give as good as you get. If a defender gets the slightest hint of fear, they will walk all over you, so I was always prepared to fight my corner. On this occasion, I fought too strong and even before I'd reached the dressing room, I knew I had made a big mistake. The manager didn't hold back, he made it clear that it was a needless sending-off. But then, I knew that.

The press went to town with it all and poked a bit of fun in my direction, which really didn't bother me. I had a good laugh to myself when I saw that one of the tabloids had mocked up a version of the film poster for *The Good, The Bad and The Ugly*. It had Jock Stein depicted as The Good, little old Colin Stein as The Bad and playing The Ugly they had our long lost cousin . . . Franken Stein. That was one of the more complimentary pieces of coverage; there was a fair bit of criticism as well for getting involved in the first place. Eddie Mulheron took a lot of stick, as the press whipped up a storm around the whole incident. There was also a lot of interest in my plans to fight the suspension, and they weren't the type of headlines I'd dreamt about making at Rangers.

I played against Aberdeen in the Scottish Cup semi-final a week later, when we dismantled the Dons in spectacular fashion. It finished 6–1 in our favour, but could have been 10 given the way we dominated, with Willie Johnston on fine form and grabbing a hat-trick.

Days later, we stuttered in the league, losing at Airdrie, and soon enough the summons to appear in front of the SFA disciplinary committee at Park Gardens dropped through my letterbox. Judgement day was approaching and I half-knew what to expect. They weren't likely to present me with a bunch of flowers, after all, so I wasn't too optimistic of a pleasant time.

I made a few visits to headquarters in my time, but it never became a comfortable place to be. It was an austere type of place, deadly quiet and almost like a school. The SFA may have bright new offices at Hampden now, but back then they were tucked away in an old townhouse, which was dark and very formal. They tried to make you feel like a naughty schoolboy going to see the headmaster.

I don't know exactly what I was expecting when I faced the committee, but I didn't anticipate the length of ban they hit me with. You get a chance to put your side of the story, but in my experience it is always a done deal, there's nothing you can do or say that is going to change their mind or encourage them to be more lenient. I knew I would end up suspended, but six weeks was a hammer-blow to me and to Rangers.

There were just seven games left in the league, coming thick and fast as the championship bounded towards its conclusion, and I was faced with the prospect of watching every one of them from the stand, not to mention the Scottish Cup final against Celtic.

I'd never felt pain and helplessness like it, and the sense of injustice started gnawing away at me as soon as the verdict was passed down. It was a moment of madness on my part, but it wasn't without provocation and the severity of the sanction was out of all proportion.

The reaction to it depended very much on which side of the Old Firm fence you sat on. Rangers supporters were outraged, Celtic fans quite content with the fact that their rivals were facing the business end of the season one man down.

Eddie Mulheron did not escape entirely. Aside from the ban

he received for his part in the clash, he became a figure of hate among our followers to the point he received death threats. I had reporters asking me what I felt about those threats, but it wasn't my place to comment on that. Nobody wants to see anyone receiving that type of abuse, but it was as if I was being held responsible and that obviously wasn't the case. I was caught up in it, but I'd done nothing to encourage it and never would. I have been on the receiving end of those types of threats myself and whether there is any intent behind them or not, it strikes real terror into your heart.

It was before an Old Firm game in 1971, the first derby after the Ibrox disaster in fact, that I was targeted. It was a very surreal experience. Linda and I were fast asleep in bed at home when we were woken in the middle of the night by hammering at the door. I got up to see who was there and found the chief constable of Lothian and Borders police and two other uni-formed officers. They asked to come in and sat the pair of us down to tell us that there had been a threat to my life. Willie Waddell had taken a phone call at the club to say what was going to happen to me and they were taking it very seriously. They conducted a thorough search of the house, keen to make sure nobody was lurking inside. Watching them search our baby's room, while Nicola was still sound asleep, was a horrible experience. They looked under her bed and in the wardrobe in her room, in case somebody was hiding in the house and it was an unwanted reminder of some of the disadvantages to being in the public eye. After they had been through every room and every cupboard, they called Waddell to let him know the house was clear and that I was safe. We had police stationed outside and they stayed with us until they were satisfied that we were not in any danger.

Obviously they had a duty to let us know what was happen-ing, but in some ways it would have been better not to know because I would be lying if I said I wasn't shaken. When you are told there's somebody out there who wants you dead, it sends a shiver down your spine. As an Old Firm player, you get used to a certain level of hatred spilling down from the terraces but, generally, that gets left behind at the ground.

Yes you also have to become accustomed to getting a bit of flak in the street or out on the town, but it tends to be the type of thing you can brush off. When it is a case of death threats, it moves to a whole new level. I'm big enough and ugly enough to look after myself, but I had a wife and young family at home and the thought that my job, or more specifically the colour of shirt that I wore, put them at risk was a big weight on my mind.

Having the police at the house provided peace of mind, but once they had gone I was still looking over my shoulder for a good few weeks. I know Linda was the same, listening out for the slightest noise at night and wondering who was out there.

Fortunately, nothing came of it and in time we got back to life as normal, but the situation certainly hammered home what it meant to live under the microscope, so I can sympathise with the way Mulheron must have felt when he was the one in the firing line.

The strength of feeling was understandable. It did not take long for the conspiracy theories to surface and the make-up of the disciplinary committee that handled my case was central to them. The panel's chairman, and therefore the man holding the most power, was Robert Kelly, and he just happened to hold the same position at Celtic. Only Kelly could say whether club allegiance played any part in the decision-making process, because it was, and still is, something that goes on behind closed doors. The Rangers supporters had their own views and he was not a popular man in certain parts of Glasgow in the aftermath, somewhere alongside Eddie Mulheron in popularity.

I was never convinced by the conspiracy theory but would never be so bold as to claim it could not be true. After all, how many times did you see the Old Firm drawn to play each other in the early rounds of a cup competition in those days? One way or another, we always seemed to be kept apart until the showpiece final and rumours about the hot and cold balls for the draw didn't appear as outlandish as they first sounded when you actually sat down and looked at the way the knock-out tournaments panned out.

I was less concerned with the claims of an anti-Rangers conspiracy and more worried about the consequences. I dreamt of winning the league and lifting the Scottish Cup to cap a memorable first season at Ibrox and in an instant that had been snatched away from me.

There was no real appeal process, or at least not one with any real teeth, and the only way I could see out of the mess was to challenge the SFA outwith the comfort zone of Park Gardens.

For one thing, I wasn't exactly flavour of the month with the blazers. I'd been sent off a couple of times while I was with Hibs and then again just a few months after joining Rangers during a game at Kilmarnock, when I traded blows with a home player after another spate of fouls against me.

That was actually Tommy McLean's fault. He was still a Killie player at the time and he'd clattered me on the touchline, pulling his studs down the back of my leg. I was having none of it and went toe-to-toe with wee Tommy, until Billy Dickson moved in to protect Tam. Billy and I ended up having a bit of a confrontation and I was soon heading for another early bath. I ended up joining Billy in a few Scotland squads after that and we were able to have a good laugh about that day. When the red mist lifts, there's very rarely any bad blood and I had a lot of time for him.

Mind you, at the time I was cursing the man. For the sending-off at Rugby Park I was hit with a four-week ban, another heavy punishment in my eyes, but had the last laugh when the weather struck and a series of postponed games meant I ended up missing just a single match. I figured that it may not have helped my case when I rolled up in front of the committee just a few weeks later, after another sending-off. As far as they were concerned, I'd got one over them in the past and they appeared desperate to even the score.

It was suggested to me that, given the mitigating circumstances and the provocation I had faced, I would have a strong case if I was prepared to take the matter to court and initially there was support from within the club for going down that route. I stewed on it for the best part of a week and the pain didn't go away, so I decided to press ahead and go for my day in the witness stand.

I was ready to fight tooth and nail, but within days of making my mind up I was called in to speak to the vice-chairman, Matt Taylor. He told me that the club would not back me if I decided to pursue the legal challenge. While there was sympathy for me, Rangers were not prepared to put the club's reputation in jeopardy and have the proud name dragged through the courts.

That was the end of the matter, and it hurt. I'd been clinging onto the hope that there would be some way out, that the SFA would have to back down, but it was my own team who knocked that optimism out of me.

I realise now that Mr Taylor was right. A legal challenge would have done far more harm than good. Even if I had won the case, my card would have been marked. The SFA would have been waiting to throw the book at me given the slightest excuse and my every move would have been under the microscope.

Trying to appeal through the association was a non starter. I can't recall any appeal being successful because the SFA always back their referees to the hilt, so it would have been pointless.

The majority of referees were difficult to get along with, there was no communication. Tiny Wharton was the exception to the rule and I know I'm not alone in singling him out for praise. Tiny was a big character in every sense and I always appreciated the way he was willing to engage with players. He'd be the first to tell you if you were having a bad game and he wouldn't bat an eyelid if you gave him a bit of a verbal dig. The rest were far less open or willing to use their common-sense, as I discovered when I was sent off during my Hibs days for swearing at my teammate Peter Cormack. It was a ludicrous decision.

It was against that background that I had decided to take legal action against my latest ban, but after the club's intervention I had to accept my fate and try to make the best of a bad situation. I'd always had a short fuse on the park and it didn't take much to set me off. After the whole Mulheron situation, and the consequences of it, I worked hard to control myself better and try not to get as wound up. It was all part of the learning curve as a Rangers player.

To this day, I'm convinced I was dealt with on the basis of who I was, rather than for what I had done. Had I been a lower league player on a couple of quid a week, I doubt they would have batted an eyelid, but I was Scotland's most expensive footballer and it was a chance for the blazers to make a few headlines.

Once the anger had subsided, I knew I had to knuckle down and try to make the time pass as quickly as I could. I carried on training as hard as ever, keeping myself fresh and fit, despite having nothing to look forward to at the end of each week.

The only thing to break the monotony was our Fairs Cup involvement, which my suspension didn't apply to.

We lost 2–0 away to Atletico Bilbao in the second leg of our quarter-final, but still went through to the last four because of the 4–1 win we'd secured in the first leg. The game in Spain was at the beginning of April and the semi-final against Newcastle was not played until the middle of May, by which time I'd had more than a month out of competitive football.

It wasn't ideal preparation for what was the biggest tie of my career up to that point and the stakes were raised even further when John McNamee, who I'd played with at Hibs, was splattered all over the papers talking about what he was going to do me. He actually caught me in the tunnel before the first leg at Ibrox, apologising and insisting he'd been misquoted. I gave him the benefit of the doubt but would have loved to have scored that night. John was a big man and well equipped to carry out any threat he cared to, but it never came to that.

Unfortunately, we just couldn't break Newcastle down and had to settle for a 0–0 draw at home, setting up a winner-takes-all showdown at St James' Park It was a terrific spectacle, with hoards of our supporters heading south for it. The game was stopped at one point because fans were spilling onto the pitch and I'd never been involved in anything like it.

That game at Newcastle also marked the only time I ever met the late, great Bill Shankly. He gave me some quiet encouragement, though he was a man of few words. Shankly, who obviously knew all about me through his brother Bob, had a special aura. He demanded respect and he got it from everyone who crossed his path. Despite what he had to say, it was a hard night for everyone connected with Rangers.

Newcastle won 2–0 to go through to the final, going on to win the Fairs Cup by beating the Hungarian side Ujpest Dozsa, and I'm certain we would have got our name on the trophy had we managed to get past the Geordies. It was a frustrating tie because we had the squad to go all the way, but fell just short in the semi-final at a time when Scottish clubs were genuinely feared in European competition. Rangers had been in the European Cup-Winners' Cup final just a couple of years previously, Celtic had won the European Cup in Lisbon at the same time and we had some world class players in the First Division.

I laugh when I hear players and managers talking about getting into the last 16 as success in Europe. If your ambition only extends as far as that then you're as well binning your boots and looking for a new profession.

Getting beaten in the semi-final didn't feel like something to celebrate. We wanted to be in every final and we felt we had the right to win all of the competitions we entered.

Maybe if I'd been fully match fit I could have made the difference in that semi-final, and domestically it was just as tough to watch from the stands. In my absence, the team lost to Dundee United, drew against Aberdeen and took just a single point from two end-of-season games against Dundee.

That was six dropped points in seven games and that spell proved to be decisive in the championship race. Celtic came through to win the league by five points and I was left to wonder what would have happened if I had been available to play in those last few matches.

Then there was the fact that I also had to sit out the Scottish Cup final, which was heartbreaking. I'd already missed the League Cup final with Hibs because of the fire at Hampden and now my second opportunity to play on the big stage had been whipped away from me.

My absence allowed Alex Ferguson to cement his place back in the side, but it did not go to plan for him in that Scottish Cup showdown with Celtic. Davie White had detailed Fergie to mark Billy McNeill at set-pieces. Billy was a major threat for Celtic going forward, but Davie felt Fergie, who was always a tough character and a battler, was best equipped to keep him at bay.

Early in the final, Celtic won a corner and Bobby Lennox played a short one. Fergie ran out to try to break it up and before he knew what had happened, the ball had been swung over for Billy to pick his spot and put Celtic ahead and on the road to a devastating 4–0 victory.

I have no idea what would have happened if I had not been suspended, but I can say that if I had been told to stay tight on Billy McNeill, I wouldn't have allowed myself to be dragged out of position as Fergie was. If there was one thing I did, it was follow team orders to the letter. That early goal was pivotal in the whole game, since it put Celtic on the front foot and left us chasing the game.

Nobody could have predicted what followed, but the feeling of total helplessness was difficult for me to deal with, even if it was something I'd had plenty of experience of by that point. It could have been a great year, but instead we went away to lick our wounds, regroup and prepare for another shot at glory.

In between the start of the suspension and the cup final, there was the small matter of Scotland's World Cup qualifier against West Germany at Hampden. The Germans were the team we had to beat if we were to stand any chance of making the finals in Mexico the following year. We had beaten Austria in the first group match and needed to do the same against West Germany in the home game, knowing full well that taking full points at their place would be well-nigh impossible. We drew 1–1, with Bobby Murdoch scoring late to secure the point, but as expected it wasn't enough. Germany went on to top the group and book their place on the plane to Mexico, four points clear of us at the top of the table. We were the only team to take a point off them, but we had a team capable of taking two.

There were 115,000 at Hampden to watch it and I would have given anything to be out on the park in front of that crowd. The SFA had seen to it that I wouldn't play in that game, but it never dented my passion for playing for my country and when I did pull on the dark blue shirt, I savoured many memorable occasions.

7

Record breaker

A lot has happened in the past four decades, both in my life and in the world of football, but one record has remained untouched. While I am proud to be the man to hold it, I am absolutely staggered that it has stayed intact for so long.

To be the last man to score a hat-trick for Scotland is a nice feather in my cap, but as a proud patriot it is frustrating all the same. I'd quite happily surrender that particular claim to fame if it meant the national team returning to the big stage and qualifying for major championships again.

My international career is a source of great satisfaction for me, even if it is tinged with the disappointment that my personal achievements did not bring team success. I scored 9 goals in 21 appearances for my country, not a bad ratio at that level, but never did make it to the World Cup finals or the European Championships.

It would have been the pinnacle to play on the biggest stage, but I was a victim of circumstance as much as anything. My days in dark blue fell just before qualification for finals became the norm.

It all began for me during the final days of my time with Hibs. I was already the talk of the town as the speculation about my future grew, then the spotlight really began to burn bright when Bobby Brown called me into his Scotland squad for a game against Denmark in Copenhagen.

It was a big step up for me, still young and finding my feet in that type of company, I could easily have been in awe of the stars around me, but I was so swollen with pride that I never gave it a second's thought. I was humbled to have been given the opportunity to play for my country, it is something every boy dreams of.

In the mind of most people, not least the Tartan Army foot soldiers who follow their side through thick and thin, receiving that first call for your country would be the biggest occasion in the world. In reality, it is never quite like that.

I was taken aside at Easter Road one afternoon and informed that Scotland had requested my services, then told to get back to work. I was sent away with a letter telling me when and where to report for duty and while you want to shout from the rooftops and tell the world, deep down you know the call-up is the easy part and that making the team is the important bit.

I was fortunate that I didn't have to wait for my debut and was put straight in at No. 9 to face the Danes. I was a 21-year-old from outside Scotland's two major clubs, dropped in among some of the biggest names in British football. I remember thinking, 'Now you have to prove yourself.'

All of the top English sides had a Scot in their ranks and in many cases he was the main man. Billy Bremner at Leeds, Denis Law at Manchester United, George Graham at Arsenal, the list goes on and on.

Bremner was the captain for that game in Copenhagen, where we played at the neat and tidy Itraedspark. In fact, everywhere in Denmark was neat and tidy. It was a pleasant introduction to international football, a far cry from some of the more hostile environments I faced in my time. The trip brought Billy and me together for the first time since I'd been stretchered off after falling victim to one of his infamous tackles in the European tie between Hibs and Leeds the previous year.

Billy may have been small, but he was a fearsome character. I certainly didn't go in planning to settle any scores and as the days passed, I began to understand what made him tick. He may have put me on a stretcher previously, but in a funny sort of way I couldn't help but respect him. Bremner had a will to win that separates the good players from the great ones. He would stop at nothing to secure a victory and God help you if you got in the way. We ended up getting on well and he took me to one side and told me, 'If I'd known you better before I played you, I'd never have done you the way I did.' That was almost an apology, but there was no need. It was all forgotten as far as I was concerned.

Bremner was not the only big character in the side for my debut. John Greig was there as well as Ronnie McKinnon, Tommy Gemmell and Bobby Lennox. You would think they would have been treated like stars, but the playing staff were almost a side show, swamped by the amazing entourage that followed Scotland around in those days.

I don't think I've ever seen so many blue blazers in one place, with faces I couldn't begin to recognise following the national team to every port of call. We had representatives from every club with us, from Albion Rovers up. It was staggering when you think of the expense the SFA incurred, but I don't suppose it will ever change. Football's gravy train will always attract passengers.

The game itself was relatively straightforward, although we were made to work for our 1–0 win. We were sent out and left to our own devices, far removed from the approach at club level. It was a nice break from the old routine to be able to play off the cuff, not giving a second thought to tactics or game plans.

Bobby Lennox scored with 20 minutes to go and even though it was a friendly, we took a bit of stick for not making a more convincing job of it. The Scandinavian countries were not considered to be in the same league as their British counterparts, so the supporters expected better than a one-goal win. Now the roles have been reversed and the likes of Denmark have stolen a march on us, especially technically.

I felt I did well and settled into international football comfortably enough. Peter Cormack, my Hibs strike partner, came on in the closing stages. Having him around in the days leading up to the game was a bonus for me. Peter had been in and around the squad for a few years, making his debut against Brazil at Hampden in 1966, and told me lots of tales from that day. We had a great relationship at club level, so having a good friend in the squad for the Denmark game settled my nerves and, no matter how fleetingly, it was a great feeling to be leading the line alongside him in a Scotland shirt.

By the time I pulled on the jersey again, I was a Rangers player and even more at ease, with plenty of colleagues from Ibrox to keep me company. I know a lot of people claim that playing for the Old Firm gives you an advantage when it comes to winning caps, but I don't see it that way. Scottish football is a peculiar environment, with the big two pretty much getting their pick of the best players, so it stands to reason that Rangers and Celtic end up with the best talent and therefore the bulk of the internationals.

I'd been at Rangers for a month or so when I made my second Scotland appearance, playing in my first competitive game for my country. It was a World Cup qualifier away to Cyprus and it's true what they say about it being a small world. As we were sitting on the bus in Nicosia, heading for the game, a supporter jumped on board and started pointing at me. He shouted, 'Hey you, Stein, it's my brother that should be in the team, not you.' It turned out to be the brother of a guy called Davie Marshall, who had played for Linlithgow Rose and Airdrie. You can take the boy out of West Lothian, but you'll never get away from it.

That game in Cyprus was played on an ash park. It was December, but it was still brick hard and wouldn't take a stud. Then there was a deluge of rain before kick-off that softened the surface just in the nick of time. Had we played on what was effectively concrete, it could have been a different story. You are always on a hiding to nothing against the international minnows, but if you concentrate and do the simple things right, it should never be a problem.

There was a big British Army presence in Cyprus and a significant Scottish contingent within the forces, so our support was strong. There were thousands cheering us on and we didn't disappoint, rattling in five goals before half-time to put us out of sight of the Cypriots. The game ended 5–0 and even although we took our foot off the pedal after the break, it was a professional performance. I scored the fifth, just a couple of minutes before half-time, to open my international account.

It was a solid result in our World Cup qualifying campaign but frustratingly, I had to sit out the all-important first game against Germany because I was still suspended.

It was after missing that match against the Germans early in 1969 that I started off on a five-game scoring run, kicking off in the 5–3 home international win against Wales at the Racecourse Ground in Wrexham.

That day, we had Tommy Lawrence in goal for us and it was like something from a comedy show. He kept going for balls and missing them. Wales must have thought all their Christmases had come at once. Lawrence was Liverpool's goalkeeper so he must have had some pedigree, yet any time I played with him for Scotland he was an accident waiting to happen.

In that game against the Welsh, he was replaced at half-time by Jim Herriot, who was with Birmingham City at the time. It was 2–2 at that point, with Billy McNeill scoring early and my goal after around quarter of an hour keeping us all square. Alan Gilzean, Billy Bremner and an own goal won us the match.

I made it two goals in two games when we played Northern Ireland at Hampden three days later, notching a second-half equaliser, but for the first time in my career scoring was just a side issue. That day I lived the dream: I played alongside Denis Law.

To play with the Law Man was one my great ambitions and to

realise it was huge for me. Denis oozed charisma from every pore. His enthusiasm rubbed off on everyone around him and even though he was coming to the end of his career his ability never faded. He still had the touch that made him one of the greatest players the world has ever seen.

If I could have played in one game for Scotland, that would have been the one. The thing I always come back to with Denis was how much he wanted to get one over on the English; he knew his life would be unbearable south of the border if things didn't go our way. A nicer man you couldn't hope to meet, but underneath was a real determination to win.

The game against Northern Ireland teed us up for an Auld Enemy match at Wembley the following month. We needed to win to have any hope of taking the 1969 home international crown, but unfortunately it didn't quite go to plan. We lost 4–1, but it was still one of the most memorable occasions of my life. It was my twenty-second birthday and to celebrate at Wembley was something special.

Even driving up Wembley Way in the team bus was an experience, making our way through a sea of Scotland fans. It looked like Scots had taken over London and the only Englishman I saw on the journey was Rod Stewart dressed in his tartan suit and shouting for us. In the old Wembley stadium, the teams ran out from behind the goals and when we did that there was just a wall of colour to greet you, the Lion Rampant flags waving at you from the far stand and Saltires in amongst them.

I'll always remember turning to Jim Herriot in the tunnel and seeing him staring back with strips of thick black boot polish under each eye, just like the American footballers wear. He told me it was to cut out reflection from the lights and help him catch high balls. The theory was great, the practice not quite so good and within 20 minutes we were 2–0 down through Martin Peters and Geoff Hurst. Mind you, maybe without the boot polish it would have been six.

A couple of minutes before half-time, I got in on the act and the noise from the Scotland fans in the crowd made the hairs stand up on the back of my neck. People talk about the Hampden roar, but the reaction to a Scotland goal at Wembley is difficult to beat.

It put us right back in the game, but England pulled away from us in the second half with another couple of goals from Peters and Hurst. They had a pretty handy team that day, with Gordon Banks in goal and Bobby Moore at the back. Then there was Alan Ball and Franny Lee in midfield, not to mention Bobby Charlton and Geoff Hurst leading the line. We saw how good they were at the World Cup in Mexico the following year, when they would have won it had it not been for a special Brazil team standing in their way.

Moore was a star in the World Cup finals, and that was no surprise to me. I played against him on a number of occasions and he was a real tough customer. I played against Franz Beckenbauer more than once, too, and they were very difficult to separate. Moore did not have the same attacking instincts as the Kaiser, he was a defender through and through, but he may just have edged it when it came to picking the better player between the two of them.

It was difficult to get much change out of either of them, although I did walk away with Beckenbauer's jersey after one of the internationals. He didn't get one of mine, swapping was strictly off-limits for us. If I'd have tried it with Rangers, Willie Waddell or Jock Wallace wouldn't have been shy about getting you to march into the opposition dressing room to ask for your kit back. They were always careful with the pennies.

People think of Beckenbauer as unflappable, but I always have a wry smile to myself when I think back to our games against each other. I liked to give defenders a bit of stick and nine times out of ten they rose to the bait. Even the Kaiser did, and I can say for sure that certain swear words are the same in German as they are in English after our little exchanges. I always figured that if a player was caught up in a few verbals, they wouldn't be focused on their job, so if I could wind them up, I'd have an advantage.

Maybe that's where the urban myth about my nickname comes from. For as long as I can remember, I've been known as Louis, or Louis The Lip in full. A lot of people think it was down to comparisons with Muhammad Ali, or the Louisville Lip as he was known. I was cocky like Ali right enough, but the real story behind the nickname's a lot less glamorous. It was actually Bobby Duncan at Hibs who christened me with that name after I turned up at Easter Road with a big scab on my lip. The ribbing I took that day stuck and ever since then I was called Louis on every training field and pitch I played on.

Moore and Beckenbauer were the toughest international defenders I faced. Unfortunately for poor Cyprus, they didn't have anyone of the same calibre and the game against them at Hampden turned out to be the stuff dreams are made of.

It fell just a week after our defeat at Wembley in May 1969 and everything I touched that day turned to goals. They actually frightened us a few times early in the game, but after Eddie Gray scored in the fifteenth minute it turned into one-way traffic. Despite the final score, the visiting keeper actually earned his corn with plenty of impressive saves, but it takes more than one man to stop a team and there wasn't much resistance from anywhere else.

Billy McNeill made it 2–0 before I gave us a three-goal lead at half-time with a headed goal from a Charlie Cooke corner. It was my first experience of playing alongside Cooke, and what an absolute pleasure that was. Charlie was a wild man in those days, although I gather he's changed his ways and hasn't touched a drop of drink for years. I knew him as a party animal but a sublime player into the bargain. He was a great character to have around the squad and a huge bonus on the park. He had tremendous ability on the ball, not to mention defence-shredding vision, and it is little wonder he became such a hero at Chelsea. He's one former teammate I'd love to catch up with.

The Cyprus players were all part-timers and after the break we ripped them to pieces. Just a couple of minutes after changing ends, I struck my second goal when I nipped in front of the keeper to pick up on a slack pass back and took it past him to walk it into the net.

I secured my hat-trick when the clock hit the hour mark, this time with a volley from a cute cross by Willie Henderson. With guys like Cooke and Henderson around, the chances always flow thick and fast. I was fortunate to play alongside some really top-class wingers, both for club and country, and for a goal-scorer it is heaven to receive that type of service.

The other great advantage that day was having Alan Gilzean alongside me. Alan joined Spurs for a pretty penny from Dundee in 1964 but he was good value. He had a real knack for hanging in the air and when you were playing up with him, you didn't have to challenge for any balls in the air. You just left them for him to win, and more often than not he did exactly that.

A couple of minutes after scoring my third, I grabbed another goal, a net-buster from a tight angle after the keeper had parried Eddie Gray's shot, and I thought I was destined to get a fifth before the game was out.

Willie Henderson had already made it 7–0 when we won a penalty in the closing stages. It was down at the Rangers end, where a lot of the 40,000 crowd were stationed, and they were chanting my name, willing me to take it. I was desperate to give them what they wanted and had the ball in my arms, ready to spot it up, when Tommy Gemmell marched up and snatched it away. He was the designated penalty-taker and clearly wasn't happy that I was planning to ignore team orders. I was speech-less, just shooting a few daggers in his direction, but nothing I could have said would have changed his mind.

He would never have realised it, but Tommy actually did me

a favour. With four goals, my confidence must have been bubbling over because I would never normally jump to the front of the queue to take a penalty. The truth is, I was never a dead-ball specialist, whether it was free-kicks or penalties, I preferred to leave them to the experts, apart from a stint at Coventry when I took it upon myself to volunteer. Big Tommy tucked the penalty away to make it 8–0 and I had to content myself with the four goals. I suppose I shouldn't be greedy, especially when you consider how rare Scotland hat-tricks have proved to be.

When you hold records it isn't a case of keeping a chart on the wall and ticking off every time somebody tries to beat it. I didn't even realise I was the last to score in five consecutive games until the journalist Rodger Baillie came out to interview me about it in 2005 for *The Times*. Kenny Miller had scored in three consecutive games and was going for a fourth, so Rodger, one of the old guard in Scottish journalism, trudged onto the building site I was working on to talk to me about it. If he hadn't told me about the record, and the fact that nobody has scored more than two goals for Scotland since my four against Cyprus, I'd never have given it a second thought. Now, I'm just waiting for the call from the press to talk about somebody matching those statistics and I sincerely hope it happens soon, it's about time the Tartan Army had something to shout about.

The fifth and final goal in the run came in September 1969 against the Republic of Ireland at Dalymount Park in Dublin, where Bohemian play their games.

I scored inside the first 10 minutes and everything happened quickly that day. For one thing, we lost goalkeeper Ernie McGarr long before half-time through injury.

We had some interesting keepers at that time. Tommy Lawrence was just too small, Jim Herriot you could probably argue the same. Then there was Ernie, who must have been the one they were looking at when they coined the phrase, you have to be mad to be a goalkeeper. Ernie would throw himself at anything, whether he thought he could get the ball or not, and whether it meant getting a boot in the head or not. He fell into some scrapes off the park as well, as the great story about him and his Aberdeen teammates Joe Harper and Willie Garner joyriding in a snowplough suggests.

The game against the Republic was a warm-up for our big World Cup qualifier against the Germans in Hamburg that year. It was win or bust for us, even at that stage in the campaign. We knew that if we wanted to make the finals we had to take something from the game in Germany, but it was never going to be easy.

We made a good fist of it, however, Jimmy Johnstone making a dream start when he scored just minutes after the first whistle. Germany pegged us back to all square at the break and despite Alan Gilzean's goal in the second half, we lost 3–2. It was a barnstorming game to play in, with the efficiency and athleticism of the Germans matched by our energy and commitment.

Mind you, I never did receive a cap for it. I've got three Scotland caps despite playing 21 games, one for each of the home international tournaments I played in. There were no mementoes for individual matches and certainly none for playing against overseas teams, only home international opposition counted.

The narrow defeat in Germany was a bitter blow to our World Cup hopes, but the defeat against Austria before the end of 1969 put the lid on it. By then, it was all about building for the future.

We had a good home international championship in 1970, beating Northern Ireland then drawing against both England and Wales, and carried that into the European Championship qualifier against Denmark at the end of the year. Unfortunately, we also lost to Belgium and then in the return against the Danes,

so I could feel another championship finals slipping away
from me.

The game in Denmark was part of a mini tour which took us
to Moscow to face the USSR, my first duck behind the Iron
Curtain. It was a real eye-opener, and such a contrast from
Copenhagen, where we had been just a few days earlier. Even in
those rather stark surroundings, the morale was good and it gave
me a chance to test my sales technique.

International football is also great for a bit of networking.
Players swap stories about their clubs, managers and teammates,
and inevitably a bit of unofficial tapping goes on. Tommy
McLean, when he was still with Kilmarnock, came to me during
the trip to Russia to ask if he should come to Ibrox and I had no
hesitation in saying yes. Mind you, he knew Willie Waddell well
enough from their time together at Kilmarnock to make up his
own mind. It happens all the time, not necessarily instigated by
clubs, either. You find your head being turned by tales from
different clubs and different countries, not least when it was the
likes of Bremner and Law talking about life at Leeds and
Manchester United. In the end, Tommy went with his heart
and confirmed the move, while still part of the Scotland party on
that trip. It was a new start for Tommy and for Scotland, too, a
big change was on the horizon.

8

Pride of Scotland

Rio de Janeiro, the Copacabana, Sugarloaf Mountain and the Maracana. That's what international football should be all about and it was the great Tommy Docherty who handed me the golden opportunity to sample the beautiful game Brazilian-style in the summer of 1972. Having been to Russia on my previous tour of Scotland duty, the next one could not have been in starker contrast. Rather than the gloom and depression of the Soviet Bloc, the South American adventure was a brilliant mix of sun, superstars, glamour and, thanks to Doc's involvement, laughter.

Scotland had been invited to compete in the Brazilian Independence Cup and for many of our players at that time it was the closest we had been to playing in an international tournament on foreign soil. Obviously it didn't have the kudos of the World Cup finals or the European Championships, but given the setting, the prospect of taking part was an attractive one for the SFA and their new manager.

Tommy had succeeded Willie Ormond on the back of Scotland's failure to make it to the European finals and was a big break from the norm for the suits at Hampden. They had always gone with the safe option in the past, but Doc was so far from that it was untrue. Somehow I can't picture him sitting in an SFA committee room making polite conversation; he was quite frankly the biggest piss-taker I've ever encountered. I liked him, though.

The Brazilians tagged the tournament the Minicopa and set it out in a World Cup format, with qualifying groups leading to knock-out stages. It was tied in with the celebrations to mark the one hundred and fiftieth anniversary of Brazil's independence from Portugal and was a big deal for them, with 19 international teams involved as well as a select side from the CONCACAF region.

We were spared the first stage of qualifying, so didn't have to fly out to South America until the end of June. That gave us the chance for a decent break at the end of our club season. I'd signed off in the European Cup-Winners' Cup final in Barcelona the month before, so I was still on a high when I was called into the Scotland squad for the tour.

After we had been told about the trip a few players began to drop out, which was a shame. I know a few weeks far from home to play friendlies isn't at the top of everyone's list of priorities, but I've also believed that playing for your country is an honour and should be treated that way. Even with the call-offs, there was a good squad of players put together, spearheaded by Denis Law. He was a veteran by then, but Denis was a class act and brilliant to have around the squad. Whatever time of day and wherever you were, you'd find him more often than not sipping on a cup of tea and holding court. He's a captivating personality. Denis was the star of that squad, but there was quality right the way through, including Billy Bremner and George Graham.

We were gathered together at the Inverclyde training centre in Largs in the 10 days building up to the tournament and put through our paces by Doc and the trainer, Ronnie McKenzie, which included some pretty brutal circuit-training to get the legs going again after the summer holidays. Doc also liked to do a lot of work with the ball and we played smaller-sided training games to mix things up.

There was a lot of hard work but many smiles as well because the manager liked to keep things light, nobody was too big a name to be cut down with a one-liner. Tommy commanded respect because he was such a forceful character, and the South American trip was entertaining to say the least.

We flew out to Brazil a week before our opening game and were based in Rio, staying in a hotel just off the Copacabana Beach. It was a little bit different from the sands down in Ayrshire, full of noise and excitement. Right into the night there were kids on the sand playing football, with just a few lamps around them to see by. It isn't until you have visited South America that you realise why they have produced so many sublime players. From the moment they can walk, boys in Brazil start mastering the ball and to see them barefoot doing their stuff is humbling.

I used to play a lot of tennis and we killed time in Rio on the courts. I'll never forget one of the kids who was tending the net for us, a boy no older than 10, rolling a tennis ball back with his foot and flicking it up before juggling it as if it was a balloon. As the international footballer, it was only right I showed him how the professionals do it but I couldn't get it off the ground. I slunk back to the tennis before I embarrassed myself any further!

We weren't there for rest and relaxation mind you, we were there for the football. We were the only home nation involved, although the Republic of Ireland played in the first qualifying round. The Irish lost out, with Portugal going through from their group. Argentina were another side who moved forward from the first set of qualifying games and Yugoslavia were the team that progressed to join us in our group.

We were in a pool with the Yugoslavs, Brazil and Czecho-slovakia. Our first game was in Belo Horizonte, a couple of hundred miles from Rio and a big sprawling city. The Brazilians didn't seem to do small, with the Mineirao Stadium a massive venue with room for more than 120,000 fans. Not surprisingly, there were only a few thousand in that day. I was watching from the bench and my chances of playing in the showpiece game against the Brazilians later in the tour weren't helped when Lou

Macari, who I was competing with for a place in the team, scored both of our goals in a 2–2 draw in strength-sapping heat. Before we left Scotland we were paraded in our new lightweight Umbro strips specially commissioned for the games in Brazil, but we would have needed built-in air-conditioning to keep us cool out there!

I sampled the humidity for myself a few days later when we took on the Czechs and I had the bizarre experience of coming on as a substitute to replace my hero Denis Law. That match was down in Porto Alegre in the Estadio Beira-Rio, right on the banks of the huge lake in the city. Czechoslovakia had set the cat among the pigeons when they held Brazil to a 0–0 draw in their opening game, something that the hosts and their fans hadn't been expecting. They were a really well-drilled side and we ran up against the same problems as Brazil, finding it impossible to break them down. The Doc threw me on in the second half to give us some fresh legs, but it ended in a frustrating goalless draw and meant we needed to take something from our match against the Brazilians to qualify for the knock-out stages. There's nothing like a challenge to focus the mind.

Although I was on the bench, it was still a phenomenal experience to be part of a squad for a match at the Maracana. It is the most spectacular stadium I have ever seen, it just towers up above you. There were somewhere in the region of 130,000 fans in when we were there, but the ground had seen crowds of 200,000 in its time. It was still pretty new when we visited, finally finished in 1967 after almost 20 years of construction. Everything about the Maracana is huge, even the dressing rooms are like football pitches. There was no Pele that day, but they did have the likes of Jairzinho, Tostao and Rivelino to call upon.

In the end, we lost by a single goal and it was the home team who went through as group winners along with Yugoslavia, who finished second after beating the Czechs in their last game.

The tournament's other final qualifying group included

Portugal, Argentina, the Soviet Union and Uruguay. The Portuguese came out on top, but lost in the final to Brazil, so there was a happy ending for the fanatical support in Rio.

Tommy Docherty was in his element out there, amongst all the flamboyance and exuberance. It's a crying shame that Tommy didn't have longer to see what he could do with Scotland because I'm convinced he would have achieved great things, his style of management was well-suited to an environment where there were lots of big-name stars. He knew how to handle us, but beneath the brilliant man-management was a very astute football mind.

As it happened, the Brazilian expedition was one of the Doc's final acts as Scotland boss and he left for Manchester United later that year. He went with 7 wins from 12 international matches chalked against his name, possibly the best record of anyone, especially when you consider that spell included matches not just against Brazil but also against Eusebio and his Portugal team.

Tommy moving on effectively signalled the beginning of the end for my own international career. Willie Ormond came in and although I made a few appearances for him during my Coventry City days, I knew I was being edged out of the picture. Lou Macari had been brought into the team by Tommy and Willie stuck with him. Although Lou was a different type of player from me, there was only room for one of us and it was his time.

I travelled the world as a Scotland player and gave every manager my all. Bobby Brown, my first Scotland boss, was very much a suit and tie character, a figurehead more than somebody in the thick of things. Bobby was a Rangers man, a legend at Ibrox from his days as the goalkeeper behind the famous Iron Curtain defence in the 1940s and 1950s. I had a soft spot for him because of that, but I don't know if he really had everybody on side in the same way as Doc. He was a schoolteacher by profession and came into the Scotland job in the late 1960s after managing St Johnstone, hardly a high-profile way to cut your teeth in coaching. The SFA obviously rated him very highly, but just as the Rangers job was maybe too big for Davie White, taking charge of Scotland was a big ask for Bobby. He ended up taking the flak for our failure to qualify for the World Cup in 1970 and the European Championship two years later and was sacked. The manner of it hurt him more than the act itself, I remember he made a great play of asking for an explanation from the SFA when the inevitable happened. As far as I'm aware, that was the end of Bobby Brown and football, certainly at the top level.

By bringing in Tommy Docherty, the SFA had gone for the polar opposite. Bobby was quiet and unassuming, Tommy loud and brash. Bobby was always well turned-out in a tailored suit and tie, Tommy was far more comfortable getting a tracksuit and boots on with a stopwatch round his neck.

When Doc left for Old Trafford, the SFA were presented with a problem. The solution was Willie Ormond, somebody whose personality and methods were smack bang in the middle of Brown and Docherty. Ormond was more involved than Brown had been, but not as strong as Docherty. Willie would turn to the likes of Billy Bremner and just say, 'You know more about the opposition than anyone, you take over.' And Billy would do the rest of the team talk, giving us the low-down as he saw it. Maybe that was a lack of authority, but in the scheme of things it made sense.

There was a lot of experience in that dressing room and a lot of big personalities, people who were club captains with major sides. There was Bremner of Leeds, Greig of Rangers, McNeill of Celtic. The great thing was that although they were all leaders, there were no egos to contend with, there was never any tension in the camp. For home matches, we'd take over the Queen's Hotel in Largs and I loved the international get-togethers, where the camaraderie was superb.

My final game in Scotland colours was at least a big one. I played the last 20 minutes or so of a home international at Wembley against England in the summer of 1973. By then, Kenny Dalglish, a player Tommy Docherty had brought into the Scotland fold initially, was established on the scene. Joe Jordan was also in favour, so the manager had plenty of options to choose from in the forward positions.

Every dog has their day and when the call-ups ended, it didn't come as a major shock to me. For the first couple of squad announcements you wait and hope your name is on the list, but then you accept it and move on. Of course, I would like to have won more caps, but international football is a step up and if you aren't at your peak then there's no point being there. As a finisher, I was always supremely confident, but my pace was probably beginning to fade. Speed is the one thing you need more than anything at that level.

I'd had a good innings, played lots of games and scored my share of goals, not to mention setting a couple of records along the way. To have played in a major championship would have been wonderful, but I can't complain too much. When you consider that the likes of George Best and Ryan Giggs never got their shot at the World Cup, you realise nobody has a divine right to play on that stage.

Tommy Hutchison went to the 1974 World Cup while we were teammates at Coventry. He had a big Vauxhall Victor and threw me the keys before he left because his wife couldn't drive, so I did get a World Cup bonus of sorts!

It was an odd sensation, watching the 1974 finals as a Scotland supporter rather than playing, but I was never bitter about it. Whether in the squad or not, all I have ever wanted is to see Scotland doing well. That's why nobody will be happier than me when my international records fall.

9

Changing of the guard

At international level I played under three very different managers, and my club career was similar. I worked for a succession of different men with different approaches to the game and to their handling of players, so I became almost immune to change when it happened. Managers moving on becomes part and parcel of professional life, but sometimes those events hurt.

Davie White was the man who showed more faith in me than perhaps any other manager in my career. He put his neck on the line to sign me and moved heaven and earth to make it happen. When he was sacked in 1969, it cut me to the bone. As far as I was concerned, there was no warning, no big build-up. One day he was the boss and the next he was gone, wiped from Ibrox as if he had never been there.

The circumstances were unusual to say the least, as White was replaced by his fiercest critic, Willie Waddell. The Deedle, as Waddell was known inside and outside of Rangers, was a playing legend at Ibrox. His credentials stood up to the closest scrutiny. As a manager he also had a solid track record, having guided unfancied Kilmarnock to the Scottish championship in 1965. He quit Killie to take up a role as a football writer with the *Daily Express* and it was from that position of power that he manoeuvred his way into the Rangers manager's office.

Media criticism in normal circumstances can be brushed aside, a matter of opinion that fans can agree with or disregard as they please, but when it comes from somebody with Waddell's authority, it is like a hammer-blow. He was a wily old fox;

you only have to look at the timing of his managerial exits to see that. At Kilmarnock, he got out when the going was good, not long after winning the league championship, and at Rangers he moved upstairs in the wake of the European Cup-Winners' Cup success in 1972. Waddell was no mug and everything he did was carefully planned. I don't think his criticism of White was any less orchestrated and in the cold light of day, it is plain to see it was perfectly executed.

The Deedle did not hold back when it came to analysing White and his team. When your manager is getting it in the neck, it is impossible not to take it personally; after all, it wasn't White who was out there on the field. Every round of criticism fired in his direction included a few bullets towards the players and it felt as though we were easy targets.

The previous season, under Davie White, could have been one of the greatest for the club. We should have won both the Fairs Cup and the Scottish Cup, and I'm convinced the league title would have been in touching distance if I hadn't sat out the tail-end of the 1968/69 campaign through suspension in the wake of the Eddie Mulheron incident.

The board, who sanctioned my signing and the investment that went with it, clearly still trusted their manager's judgement, because they allowed him to bring Alex MacDonald on board in another big-money deal. Doddie cost around £50,000, but nobody could question White's judgement because he proved himself worth every penny and more.

Yet according to the papers, and that one important journalist in particular, that last season was a shambles and the next threatened to be the same. It was exaggerated beyond belief, but it made good copy. If the media had been waiting for an excuse to put the final nail in the manager's coffin then they were handed the perfect one just three months into the 1969/70 season.

The campaign didn't get off to the textbook start when we

failed to make it out of the group stage of the League Cup, having been drawn alongside Celtic in our pool. We beat them in the home game, but a draw at Ibrox against Raith proved to be our undoing and it was Jock Stein's team who progressed. Before a ball had even been kicked in the league, we were on the back foot and a couple of early defeats in the First Division, against Celtic and Ayr, didn't help matters.

We recovered well enough and negotiated a tricky European Cup-Winners' Cup first-round tie against Steaua Bucharest to set up what was considered to be a far easier second-round double-header against Gornik Zabrze.

Davie White was assured and confident going into the games. He was adamant we had far too much firepower for the Poles and wanted us to go at them from the start. Nobody could have predicted what happened next.

We were beaten 3–1 in the first leg, away from home, and were well and truly caught on the hop. I have only ever seen Ronnie McKinnon beaten for pace on two occasions and they came in our two matches against the Polish side. Gornik had a player by the name of Wlodzimierz Lubanski who was frighteningly quick. He left big Ronnie for dead, which is one hell of an achievement. I played against the big man often enough while I was with Hibs to know he was like lightning, you couldn't chase him down and if you looked over your shoulder and saw him closing in you knew it was time to get a shot away fast. Yet the Pole was his match.

We expected to claw it back in the second leg, but things went from bad to worse. We fell 3–1 at Ibrox to go out 6–2 on aggregate and before we were even washed and changed, the fans had gathered outside the main stand.

They were calling for the manager's head on a plate, no doubt egged on by the coverage the papers had been giving us. When you have supporters protesting in the street it's obvious there are problems, but because we had faith in our own ability there was never a question in my mind that we would turn the corner and start winning trophies.

Despite what was going on around us, I don't think anyone expected the speed with which everything unravelled. Rangers were not a sacking club. Scot Symon, prior to White, had been the first boss to get the bullet and most people expected that the furore surrounding that would have meant the board would not go down the same road in a hurry. Or so we thought. When we arrived the following day, the manager had been dismissed. We were gathered together to have the news broken to us and nobody was celebrating.

So often you read about a manager losing the dressing room before they are sacked, but that wasn't the case on this occasion. The perception was that senior players questioned his authority and doubted his credentials, but hand on heart I never saw any evidence of that. There was still plenty of support for White within the squad and I can't think of anyone who had a particular reason to want him replaced. Personally, I had every reason to want him to stay. He signed me and there was no guarantee that whoever came in his place would want to keep me. Given the amount of money White had spent on me, I would have been an easy target for anyone coming into the club with a point to prove.

We did not have long to wait to discover who our new gaffer would be, although I don't think any of us ever really doubted where the board would turn. Willie Waddell would be the next man in charge, of that we were sure. And so it proved, with the Deedle unveiled amid much fanfare to the press pack he had just left behind. Waddell had many friends in the media, not surprisingly, and for that reason was starting from a very good position.

Waddell was a very deep person, but what rose to the surface was his passion for Rangers Football Club. From his very first meeting with the team, it was made crystal clear what was expected of us. As far as he was concerned, it was a privilege to play for Rangers and, of course, he was right. He argued that we were treated to the very best seats in the theatre or in restaurants because of the badge we wore on our chest and that in return we should give the very best service to the club.

He had the ability to send a shiver down your spine when he spoke and what he stressed again and again was that you were a Rangers player 24 hours a day. There was no time to switch off, he wanted us to live and breathe it. We were given that message in no uncertain terms, in typically frank and forthright fashion. Waddell clearly felt his predecessor was not a disciplinarian and his first task was to set that straight even the way he tipped his glasses and peered over the top of them was like a schoolmaster addressing his class.

I felt incredible sympathy for Davie White, but at the same time I could not help but respect the new manager. He wasn't asking us to do anything he had not done himself as a player and he wasn't shy of reminding us about the success he had enjoyed during his Ibrox heyday in the 1930s and 1940s. He played more than five hundred games for the club and collected nine league medals, two Scottish Cup medals and three League Cup medals. With that type of success, there was no room for anyone to argue with Waddell and not many people tried, he was so stubborn that you knew there was no point.

Waddell pressed ahead with essentially the same team that Davie White had assembled, but he enjoyed far greater success. Perhaps White would have done the same had he been given more time, but his successor had far greater experience and clout. While Waddell introduced Tommy McLean from his old club Kilmarnock, he showed faith in the majority of the players he inherited. Those who fell by the wayside were the ones who could not meet his demands for total dedication and commitment, with Willie Henderson and Jim Baxter among the casualties. Wee Willie and Slim were hardly wallflowers and the two of them together generated fireworks more often than not. Now and again, it would spill into football and they'd roll in late for training or not in tip-top condition but, as they discovered, the new manager was not willing to put up with players who tested his patience. Willie lasted longer than Jim, but both were sacrificed eventually.

There were a few nervous individuals in the dressing room when Waddell named his first team, but there were no wholesale changes. I kept my place and soon settled into life under the new regime. It turned out to be a real test of endurance as Waddell set about stamping his authority on the squad. He brought in Jock Wallace as his right-hand man and the two of them were a formidable combination.

Jock's army background shone through from the offset and life was far from easy. The funny thing was, with his thick accent and hundred-miles-an-hour delivery, you often couldn't make out a word Jock was saying yet he still got his message across, he didn't need words to let you know what he was thinking.

The notorious trips to Gullane became part and parcel of life for us virtually as soon as Waddell and Wallace teamed up together. They would run us up and down the sands there until we dropped – it wasn't known as Murder Hill for no reason. Players would be throwing up left, right and centre, but there was no mercy. Jock would keep us running until we couldn't go on physically, and mentally it was the hardest thing I have ever encountered.

Some were better than others at getting through the ordeal. Even John Greig and Alex MacDonald, two of the fittest men I've ever played alongside, toiled. Willie Johnston was by far the best I ever saw when it came to tackling Murder Hill. Willie had incredible stamina and energy, it was as if he enjoyed the pain. It was like a game to Bud and he refused to be beaten by it.

The laugh of it is that when we were first sent to Gullane, we thought we were going for a nice day out at the seaside. We were packed off on the bus from Glasgow with not a clue of what lay in store for us. It was left to Jock to explain what was required, but actions speak louder than words and after that first trip we knew all about it. Future journeys to the east coast were an odd experience, there was obviously a sense of dread about what lay in store, but you knew there would be an amazing rush of adrenalin when you came through the other side and survived it.

For all we may have hated the pain we suffered on those marathon sessions on the beaches, it is no coincidence that many members of that squad went on to play well beyond so many of their peers. I retired young, but was very much the exception and not because I couldn't have carried on. To this day I'm convinced my good health is a lot to do with the attention that was paid to our physical conditioning all those years ago. The likes of Sandy Jardine, Alex MacDonald, Tommy McLean and many others all cruised past appearance milestone after milestone and I put that squarely at Jock's feet. He was a fitness fanatic and he had us in incredible condition.

Where it paid dividends was in the latter stages of games, and I know I was not alone in feeling we had a real edge in closing out matches. While the opposition were flagging as the clock ran down, we were just hitting top gear. I always felt supremely confident in a one-on-one situation, because I knew I had an incredible bank of strength and stamina to call upon. If you feel that confidence, it makes you gamble on things falling for you and that is when the half-chances become goals.

It wasn't just on our regular trips to Gullane that we were put through the mill. Day in and day out, whether at the Albion training ground or inside Ibrox, we were hammered. From an old army favourite such as burpies, or squat thrusts, on the terracing, to straight runs up and down the stairs at the ground, there was never any let-up from the hard work.

It was a far cry from when Davie Kinnear and Joe Craven

took training under White. Kinnear was far more relaxed and unless you wanted to push yourself, you wouldn't need to break sweat. Harold Davis was also brought in during that time to keep us ticking over, but none of them had the same devotion to physical training as Jock Wallace. The routine under White was far less regimented and nowhere near as intense except for on one notable occasion. On the night before our European tie against Gornik in Poland, the one we lost 3–1, we were run into the ground because Willie Henderson and Jim Baxter had stepped out of line and upset the coaching staff. I can't even remember what it was, it was so inconsequential, but they took offence to it and we were all punished. It was a ridiculous idea, given we had such a vital game looming. Instead of going into the game fresh, we were going in with heavy legs and tight muscles, and it was a recipe for disaster.

Maybe the key to being a good manager is having the right people around you. Waddell had Wallace and Stan Anderson and the three of them complemented each other perfectly. Willie Thornton, who had worked briefly under White, remained alongside Waddell as his assistant and he was another absolute gem. Thornton was a true gent, but he had a football brain as sharp as a pin and had a big part to play in the European success of 1972. Thornton and Waddell had come through the ranks together as young players, as winger and centre forward respectively, and their friendship lasted the test of time. They had an understanding and thought the same way about the game.

Unlike Waddell and Thornton, who were both legends in their own right, White had been plucked from relative obscurity by Scot Symon to join the Ibrox coaching staff. Symon had been impressed by what he had seen when the young coach accompanied both Rangers and Celtic in the 1966/67 European campaigns, and the young whippersnapper was no fool. Tactically, I always found him to be very astute and as a man-manager

I liked his quiet and relaxed approach. But football is a results business and there is no room for manoeuvre once you are in the thick of the Old Firm action. Waddell proved in the years ahead that he could deliver the success that White had failed to find.

That manifested itself within the new manager's first full season in charge, when we lifted the first trophy of my Rangers career. Just as the St Michael's Cup medal I won as an Armadale player meant so much to me, so too did the first of my collection as a professional. Our win in the 1970/71 League Cup actually masked an indifferent start to Willie Waddell's tenure at Ibrox, but it is amazing how well the glimmer of silver can distract even the most demanding supporters.

The League Cup was still being played on a sectional basis then, with the group games kicking off the season in August and coming thick and fast right through the month. We got through our six pool games against Dunfermline, Morton and Mother-well without defeat. In fact, we dropped just a single point when we drew 0–0 with Morton, and I'd scored four in those matches to set the ball rolling for the season.

Hibs were no match for us in the quarter-final and we won 6–2 on aggregate before brushing Cowdenbeath aside in the semi-final, winning 2–0 through a goal from myself and a Willie Johnston penalty.

After the crushing disappointment of missing out on two previous cup finals, wild horses wouldn't have kept me away from Hampden. All we had to do was get the better of Celtic and the first trophy of the season was ours.

Given my track record with big occasions, I fully intended to savour every minute of my first senior final. It didn't pan out like that and the whole thing whizzed by in a blur, so much so that I didn't even notice the shirt being pinched off my back.

The 1970 League Cup final will forever be remembered as the Derek Johnstone game, and quite rightly so.

DJ stole the show, announcing his arrival with his header to clinch a 1–0 win and land the trophy. Not a bad way to start your life as a Ranger. He had only played one game, against Cowdenbeath, up to that point and was still unknown outside Govan. To anyone who had seen him at work, it was no surprise that he grabbed centre stage.

Derek had trained with the first team for a while by the time he earned his cup final place, and having watched him at close quarters I knew what he was capable of. He was a natural player with a great touch and a quick football brain. He had physical power to go with his ability and he also had the type of aerial prowess that you cannot teach. Being good in the air isn't all about height, it's about timing, too, and being able to read the flight of the ball.

There's a wonderful image of Willie Johnston towering over Wyn Davies, one of the best centre-forwards of his generation and renowned as a dominant player, to win a header. Willie is hardly a giant, but he had the knack of timing his jump to perfection, and DJ had the same talent.

Derek scored many important goals in Rangers colours, but that one in the cup final, as a raw 16-year-old, is hard to beat in terms of sheer impact. It wasn't until I watched the highlights on television after the game that I noticed the young upstart had actually nicked my jersey. There he was celebrating with the No. 9 on his back – my No. 9. I was sitting there thinking, 'He's got my shirt.' It sounds silly, but it was a strange sensation. Having been so hung up about missing the previous two finals, I obviously didn't pay any attention to where I was on the team sheet, I was just relieved to have made it to that point without any fires or suspensions getting in the way. Unbeknown to me, I ran out at Hampden wearing the No. 10 shirt that Alex MacDonald had made his own up to that point, with Doddie picking up the No. 8 that had been left by Graham Fyfe when he dropped out of the team to accommodate DJ.

The importance of that cup final cannot be overestimated.

Celtic were the dominant force and getting one over on them, even if it was in the cup rather than the league, proved that we were still at the races.

Living through Celtic's run of nine league titles in a row was tough, but there were slivers of hope throughout the period, whether at home in the knock-out competitions or through our performances in Europe. I'll argue until I'm blue in the face that we were a match for Jock Stein's side. The difference was down to how we fared in the games against the lesser lights, not necessarily in how the Old Firm contests played out.

Our biggest failing in the league was that we could not consistently shut out teams who on paper should have posed no threat to us. We had a team brimming with quality but in the cut and thrust of Scottish league football, that is not always the key. What Celtic and Stein did very cleverly was put together two teams. They had one for the big games and another for the more meaty matches against the likes of Ayr and Clyde the kicking matches.

It was one thing playing against Rangers at Hampden and quite another to go down to Somerset Park, where the boots were flying and the mud was thick. Celtic very rarely stuttered in those games, because their manager tailored his team accordingly. He was quite prepared to sacrifice silk for steel when required, whereas we would always field what would be considered to be our strongest side regardless of the occasion.

The season we won the League Cup was a case in point. We lost a lot of league games on the road at places like Airdrie, Ayr and Falkirk. These were games we should have won, but we faltered too many times. Celtic, on the other hand, were able to grind out results whether playing well or not. In the end, the horses for courses approach served Jock Stein and his side well and ensured we had a long wait to get our hands on the league trophy.

Fortunately for morale, there were still good times to savour and we made the most of celebrations when they came our way. After the 1970 League Cup final we went back to Ibrox, where a private room was set aside for the players to take advantage of the drinks laid on for us. We had become accustomed to getting together behind closed doors after a couple of minor indiscretions in town had put paid to the previous ritual of heading out to St Enoch post-match with Messrs Henderson and Baxter at the centre of the trouble once again.

Back at Ibrox, we were safe from prying eyes or overenthusiastic supporters from both sides of the Old Firm. It suited me fine, because as soon as I'd arrived at Ibrox I discovered I just couldn't venture out on the town, the attention made it impossible.

The wonderful tea lady Lizzie Love, an Ibrox institution, looked after us with food and drink fit for a king and the atmosphere was very different from the way it was after the disappointment of the Scottish Cup final of the previous year, when the team had returned to the ground to drown its sorrows. I've never seen a group of men get as drunk so quickly as after that 4–0 Old Firm defeat, with the combination of the exertions on the park and the emotion of the occasion combining with pretty dramatic effect. This second gathering was far more enjoyable.

Once you've had a taste of success, you crave more and we sensed big things were about to happen. We had a squad that we were confident was a match for every team in Scotland and we had a manager who had proved he knew how to deliver success at a club geared from top to bottom for big occasions. What we didn't realise was that all of the optimism and excitement was about to be put into perspective in the most tragic of circumstances.

10

The Ibrox disaster

The goals, the trophies and the celebrations are not the football memories I replay in my mind every day. I can go weeks and months without giving a second thought to the biggest events in my playing career. The tragedy of the Ibrox disaster is the exception, the one thing that has touched me more than any other in my lifetime and that has been with me every step of the way since.

It is a period in my life I have never spoken about outside my close friends and family. I have been asked on many occasions to take part in programmes about the disaster or to contribute to books and newspaper articles, but it never felt right to do so. When I embarked on this project, I thought long and hard about whether I should break that public silence and I came to the conclusion that it would be impossible to give an account of my life without including my own experiences of that time.

In football, it can be all too easy to get carried away and believe your own publicity. A player's life can feel unreal, you live a cosseted existence, and a charmed one in so many ways. When the good times roll, you feel like the king of the world. Yet, as anyone who was at Ibrox on that fateful day will testify, all of a sudden the game can feel very small.

It seems so insignificant to write about the game itself, but it does help put the events of 2 January 1971 into context. It must have been one of the most uneventful Old Firm games Ibrox had ever played host to, until Jimmy Johnstone scored with seconds to play. The match looked lost, but we went up the other end pushing for an equaliser. Dave Smith swung a free-kick into the box and it fell to me; with a swing of my boot, the game was all square. The celebrations sparked up around the ground.

They were still going on when I slipped out of the ground, heading for home with my wife and content with what had appeared to be a good day at the office. I was never one for hanging around too long, so had done my usual routine of getting cleaned up and changed quickly before setting off on the road east.

It was during that journey that we first heard news filtering through on the radio about the horror that was unfolding at Ibrox. By the time we arrived back in Linlithgow, the updates were becoming more and more vivid and it was clear just how terrible the situation was. I was in two minds whether to turn the car around and head back to Glasgow, but there was nothing I or anybody else could do so I decided to carry on to the house. I can't remember the rest of that night. In fact, I wandered around in a daze for days after, feeling so utterly helpless.

As a player you inevitably strike up relationships with supporters and every single member of the squad that day had a link to at least one of the 66 victims. Mine was very close to home indeed. Margaret Ferguson, the only female fan to lose her life in the disaster, had been a guest in our house just weeks before. We didn't know her, but she had taken the time to visit with a teddy bear for our daughter Nicola, who had just been born.

It was a lovely gesture, especially since Margaret didn't live in the town. She had come through from Maddiston, halfway between our place and Falkirk, just to drop off the gift, and I guess she did not even know if we'd open the door to her. But we really appreciated it. To think that the same love of Rangers that had brought her to our door that day had cost her her life, at 18, was heartbreaking. Families were ripped apart and communities devastated by what happened that day and we should never forget those who paid the ultimate price to follow their team.

There is not a day that goes by that I don't think about it. There are constant reminders, from the smallest of things to national events. As I write this, the twentieth anniversary of the Hillsborough disaster has just taken place and I doubt there is a single Rangers fan who lived through our own tragedy who did not take time out to reflect on the terrible scenes at Ibrox when they watched the memorial at Anfield.

I can remember all too well watching television footage of Hillsborough as it unfolded. In 1971, the information took far longer to drip through and it wasn't until the morning after that the full extent of what had happened became clear.

When it did, it was like a lightning bolt hitting you. I struggled to comprehend what I was being told, it was too huge to take in. Since signing for Rangers I had bounded into Ibrox every day, eager to get through the front door and begin working.

Returning for the first time after the disaster was entirely different, filled with dread and not knowing what to think or do. It was an eerie place to be in the aftermath, with a respectful hush all around the ground and signs of the clear-up and investigation impossible to avoid. Screening was put up around the scene, but it didn't disguise what had happened, nothing could. Bodies had been brought inside to the dressing rooms, the gym and other rooms inside the main stand immediately after the game and many of the players had witnessed it. For them, it was even more difficult to return.

It required strong leadership and we were very fortunate to have Willie Waddell as a figurehead. It would have been easy for everyone connected with the club to go to pieces, but he made sure we stayed strong. The manager made it clear that we owed it to the victims to pull together and stay united. He understood our grief, and the way it affected people in different ways, but wanted us to put as brave a face on it as we could. Waddell's guidance through such a difficult time was crucial. He organised us into groups for visiting relatives of the victims and attending funerals, sometimes more than one in a day. We all wanted to be there, but knew in our hearts that nothing could ease the pain those families were suffering. The funeral of Margaret Ferguson was particularly poignant for Linda and me, a terribly sad day for us as a young couple having recently become parents to a beautiful daughter ourselves.

Through it all, I had personal torment to deal with, although obviously nothing near what the families had to face up to. I believed that it was my goal that had caused the disaster, and so did most of the country. The theory was that supporters leaving the ground had turned to try to get back in to join the celebrations and it was then that Stairway 13 collapsed.

As you would expect, I took it very hard. When you score a goal, the adrenalin rush is phenomenal and in an Old Firm game that is multiplied by ten. When the realisation struck that one of those goals could have such terrible consequences, I was racked with guilt. It felt pointless to go on. Football was an irrelevance and it was hard to imagine ever feeling the same way about scoring a goal or winning a game again. What did it matter, after all?

I was still riddled with those feelings when we attended a service at Glasgow cathedral. I was standing outside afterwards when the minister approached me and put an arm around my shoulder. He simply told me, 'It's not your fault, Colin, nobody is blaming you.' It was comforting and meant the world to me; it was what I needed to hear at a time when people were treading carefully around the subject. The silence was harder to bear than if people had been saying what they thought, good or bad.

An inquiry was ordered within days of the disaster and the preliminary findings were clear the goal was not the cause, instead it had happened minutes after the final whistle and the best guess was that a spectator had tripped on the stairway and others had fallen, with horrendous consequences. There was nowhere for fans to turn, they were trapped in an area too small to handle the numbers pouring out of the ground.

I cannot pretend that it was not reassuring to hear the experts say that the goal was not a factor. The findings did lift a weight off my shoulders but also brought the realisation that apportioning blame would never bring back the 66 who died. Perhaps if there had been a definitive explanation it would have been slightly easier to deal with, but for the families of the victims there was nothing that could be said or done to bring their loved ones back.

Through all of the funerals, visits to the 145 casualties who had been hospitalised and memorial services, we had to try to carry on as best we could, through sombre training sessions and a surreal atmosphere at the ground. Even with the stairway covered, there was no escape from what had happened. We eventually played again two weeks later, against Dundee United, but there was little appetite for it either among the players or the supporters. It was still far too raw.

We drew the game 1–1 but it must be the hollowest goal John Greig has ever scored. There was really nothing for him or the rest of us to celebrate in the circumstances. We played on and did our best to remain professional, but it was tough. The season ended in defeat for us, losing to Celtic in the Scottish Cup final replay, and it was only then that we had a proper chance to get away from football and reflect fully on the disaster.

Some good did come out of it in the way Ibrox, and other grounds for that matter, were modernised and improved beyond all recognition. There weren't even safety certificates before the disaster, but everyone sat up and took notice after that dreadful day. Safety became an obsession for the directors at Rangers in particular, and within a decade the stadium had been modernised to an incredibly high standard, with the move towards seated stands placed at the top of the agenda.

In time, a report produced by Lord Wheatley was issued and the political wheels slowly began to turn. Legislation followed in the years ahead, both in terms of stadia and crowd control, but Rangers had stolen a march. Willie Waddell made it his mission to ensure that the scenes of that day on 2 January were never witnessed again, as part of an Ibrox hierarchy that had been shocked to its core. People will often argue that the atmosphere at games has suffered with the introduction of seating. I'm not convinced that is true but, even if it is, surely any price is worth paying to avoid a repeat of such a terrible waste of life.

The safety improvements were a physical change but there was also a human aspect. The disaster brought both sides of the Old Firm together in a way that had never been seen before. Those on the outside find it hard to believe that the rivalry on the pitch does not necessarily extend beyond it, with plenty of close friendships bridging the divide.

John Greig and Billy McNeill always maintained a strong respect, while Willie Henderson and Tommy Gemmell were great mates, just as Wee Willie was with Jimmy Johnstone. The directors also had a good understanding. In fact, they would share a drink from the Loving Cup after the New Year derby each year, a lovely old piece of silverware with three handles which sits in the trophy room at Ibrox. Behind closed doors, the two clubs are not as divided as you might imagine.

Throughout both squads in that era, there were great bonds. They were needed more than ever after the disaster. It is sometimes too easy to forget that the Celtic players and supporters present that day were just as much a part of the tragedy as the Rangers contingent, they went through the same shock and dismay. We sat side by side with our Celtic counterparts at many of the funerals, up to five a day at one stage, and for a time at least, the Old Firm differences were well and truly set to one side.

Sitting down and recalling the pain we all felt at that time brings the emotion flooding back, but we walked out of the ground that day. Sixty-six devoted Rangers people did not and we must never forget that.

11

Road to Barcelona

When we returned to Ibrox after the close season break in 1971, there was a common purpose among the players. We had all taken the opportunity to deal with the events of New Year in our own way. Although the disaster was still raw, with time there was the realisation that the best way of serving the memories of those who had died was to bring success to their club.

On that basis, a successful European run in the 1971/72 season was not a luxury for Rangers, it was a necessity. After getting off to a sticky start in the domestic competitions, we had an immediate opportunity to redeem ourselves in the European Cup-Winners' Cup and grabbed it with both hands.

By the time we played Rennes in the first-leg of the first round in mid-September, we had gone out of the League Cup at the group stage and had lost the opening two league fixtures of the season 3–2, the first at Partick, the next at home to Celtic.

I'd scored in each of those two matches, but any personal satisfaction is soon whipped away if the team doesn't win. There was a lot of pent-up frustration by the time we boarded the plane for France to face Rennes. We knew we were far better than our form in Scotland suggested and had a point to prove. The manager, too, needed results. He had taken over on the back of our disappointment against Gornik, so knew better than most the impact failure to progress in the continental cups could have.

As a Rangers player, you have to go into every competition with the ambition of winning it. Second place is nothing, success is everything. As we set off on the European adventure that year it was no different but, with every campaign, it takes time for the momentum to build.

Stade Rennes represented a stuffy obstacle to overcome before we could even contemplate shooting down the big guns. The French side were not a big name by any means and a lot was made of the fact that they had only played in Europe once prior to our meeting with them, but we knew better than to be deceived by their past record. They had defeated Lyon in their national cup final, a team who themselves were no strangers to cup success at that time.

French football was strong and Marseille were beginning to dominate the league scene at the start of the 1970s. It was Marseille that Rennes had beaten in their semi-final, having overcome Monaco in the earlier rounds, so it was clear that they were no mugs.

I had never played against a French side, but we had been well warned to expect a highly organised, technical group of opponents. From that very first tie, Willie Waddell was pains-taking in his attention to detail.

It was then that he introduced his system of giving each player a mug shot of the guy they would be in direct competition with. I'd get the photo of the centre-half who would be marking me, along with as much detail about him as the manager could muster from his spying trips. By the time you ran out on the park, you knew your opposite number's inside leg measurement and there were periods in matches that a little nugget of information the boss had given you before kick-off would light up in your mind and you took advantage of it. Whether a defender didn't like being turned inside, or if another wasn't great in the air, there were chances to exploit the weaknesses Waddell had pinpointed.

Not that we had many opportunities in France, given the way Rennes shut up shop. Willie Johnston and I were put together as a forward two from the start of the European run and asked to hunt as a pair. We'd stay close together, moving from the centre into the two channels and keeping the opposition on their toes. The way we played was crucial to Waddell's game plan for European ties, with the two of us asked to drop deeper than we normally would in domestic football to pull the defenders to us and open space up behind. Willie Johnston took advantage of one of the few chances we did create in the away leg to put us ahead, but they clawed it back to 1–1 and we left with the draw, taking the French side back to Ibrox where we were clear favourites to progress with the home support behind us. The Rennes manager was highly critical of us at the time, claiming we had been overly defensive, but that was naivety on his part. He was up against a shrewd football thinker in Waddell, a man ahead of his time, and the record books show we got it right, not Rennes.

The home game was another tight affair, as we'd come to expect, but Alex MacDonald's goal took us through. We'd lost another league game, this time against Aberdeen, just days before the second-leg against Rennes, so victory had become even more important. We'd lost three of our first four matches in the First Division, but the prospect of some big European nights tempered the disappointment and there was always a sense that the league form was a temporary blip.

All of the games were played on Wednesday nights, with the draw for the next round made on the Friday after the second leg. We were all gathered at Ibrox for training when it began to filter through that we were going to face Sporting Lisbon in the second round, and there was a real buzz in the dressing room.

The destination never even enters your mind when it comes to these competitions, it is all about the opposition. I've travelled the world as a football player but rarely seen much more than the inside of an airport or hotel room during those trips. It is about work, not pleasure, and while we did have the occasional night out during the foreign sorties, there was very little time for sightseeing or mingling with the locals.

So it wasn't the bright lights of Lisbon that whetted the appetite, it was the prospect of taking on Sporting. They had won the Portuguese title the year before we played them and were regular cup winners too. In Europe, they had experienced mixed fortunes but had gone one better than Rangers by winning the Cup-Winners' Cup in the 1960s and were a real force to be reckoned with, the team peppered with international players from Brazil, Argentina and Portugal. They were a different prospect from Rennes.

While the French were all about discipline and control, Sporting had flair in abundance. We expected there would be goals over the two legs but perhaps not the twelve that followed. If there has ever been a more eventful double header in the history of Rangers, I can't recall it. The ties against Sporting had the lot: drama, excitement, tension and, for one of our team, heartbreak.

They came to our place first and it was one of those great European nights at Ibrox. There was a good crowd for the Rennes match, but for the visit of Sporting the place was packed and our fans were in great voice. We responded with a devastating performance in the first 45 minutes, probably the best spell of play in the entire run to the final in Barcelona.

I tucked away a double to add to Willie Henderson's goal and we were on easy street. Or so we thought. Sporting brought on a new left winger at the break and he started rampaging up and down that flank, giving Andy Penman a real tough time. Before we knew it, they had pegged it back to 3–2 and what should have been a breeze turned into a bit of a struggle over the finish line. Our performance merited a far more convincing result, but the key thing was that we were heading to Portugal with the advantage and all we had to do was shut them out to take us through. Keep it tight, not give anything away and we were home and dry. To say the second leg didn't go to plan is an understatement, it turned into a nightmare from start to finish and a trip that in the end we were just glad to see the back of.

The omens weren't good when our plane from Glasgow was grounded due to a strike in the air traffic control service. We ended up having to travel via London, first flying into Heathrow and then having to dash across the capital to Stansted for a connection to Europe. When we got to the airport, there were even more problems and we ended up having to stay in London overnight before flying out in the oldest and shakiest plane I'd ever clapped eyes on.

We were late into Portugal, just within Uefa's 24-hour deadline for visiting teams to arrive, and it meant that our preparations were shot to pieces.

It was a shambolic start to the trip and the game mirrored that. I equalised twice after we'd fallen behind early in each half. Peter McCloy didn't have his best game that night and by the time the 90 minutes had passed we were 3–2 down on the night and level at 5–5 on aggregate. Willie Henderson put us back in front in extra time, but they were a resilient bunch and brought it back to 6–6 on aggregate, 4–3 on the night, with a penalty by the end of the 120 minutes. Sporting had drummers along one of the touchlines and it was a sensational environment to play in, full of passion and intensity.

In between all of that there was the horrific injury to Ronnie McKinnon. One of the Sporting players went right over the top of the ball with around two minutes to play, going for the man 100 per cent, and nailed his target. Ronnie fell to the ground and I was one of the first to reach him. His leg was straight but his toes were facing the ground, it was a sickening sight. I slid my hand down his leg to try and assess the damage but it was just soft – the bone had gone, shattered by the Portuguese hatchet man.

I snapped, going straight at him. John Greig wasn't far behind, as the whole Rangers team flew into a rage. By the time the referee calmed things down, the Sporting management team had substituted their man and it was just as well they did. I fully intended to do him serious damage, something I'm not proud of in hindsight, but the anger was boiling up inside me. I've never had the longest fuse, but in football I never set out to hurt an opponent. I'd protect myself and give as good as I got, but nothing more sinister than that. There in the Jose Alvalade Stadium, I was ready to break the habit of a lifetime and deliberately take out an opponent – it was going to be an eye for an eye as far as I was concerned and I've no doubt a few others felt the same. Fortunately, the Portuguese dugout was wise to it and saved us all the prospect of ugly scenes.

I roomed with Ronnie and we had become great friends. To see him being carried from the park after such a horrible assault was hard to take. He put a brave face on it, but we all knew how bad it was and how much pain he was in. Ronnie spent the night in hospital and I went back after the game to an empty room, packing up all his gear for the flight home the next day. It was a night when we should have been celebrating qualification for the quarter-finals of the competition, but it was a lonely one for me, wondering if Ronnie's injury was as serious as it looked.

His leg was not put in a cast until we got back to Glasgow and he was stretchered onto the plane, with room made across a couple of rows of seats to lay him down.

Ronnie was a confident character and brave, too, but the injury effectively ended his career at Rangers. He was a wonderful servant to the club and immensely successful, but it must have torn him apart to have to watch the Barcelona run from the sidelines. As with all long-term casualties, he was still involved with the squad day-to-day, but it can't be the same when you're not able to take part. When he did return to fitness, around a year later, Ronnie was given a free transfer and headed to South Africa to rebuild his life and career.

That night in Lisbon marked the end of his involvement in

the competition and the start of Dave Smith's. They were horrendous circumstances for Dave to be introduced, considering that he was just coming back from a broken leg himself. I'll never forget watching Dave come on to take Ronnie's place and seeing him looking as white as a sheet. Here was a man who had overcome two broken legs watching a friend and colleague being carried off in agony. Dave would have been hoping to ease his way back in, but instead he was thrown into the most bizarre of games.

The manager came up with a masterstroke by putting Dave Smith in as sweeper. He was an unlikely defender, given that he would be the first to admit he just didn't tackle, but what he had was tremendous vision and a range of passing that could slice teams in two. He was always paired with a centre-half who did the dirty work, with Colin Jackson and then Derek Johnstone put in to attack the high balls and close down the attacks on the ground. That left Dave free to hoover up the crumbs and set about turning defence into attack, away from the congestion of midfield.

It was practically unheard-of at the time, with perhaps only Franz Beckenbauer with the German international team playing as a sweeper in the same way.

Whether Waddell had copied that from the Germans I'm not sure, but in European football it worked like a dream. With Bud and me pulling the opposition all over the place, Dave and the midfielders had spaces to aim for and to spring quick counter-attacks. The system came into its own as the ties went on, but in Lisbon there was no pattern to what took place.

After the game ended 6–6 on aggregate, the referee signalled for penalties. I knew it was wrong and rounded on him, explaining that the away goal rule was in force and in our favour. He spoke English well enough but just wouldn't entertain what I had to say, he was adamant it was time for penalties.

Grudgingly, we took part in the shoot-out and messed it up in spectacular fashion. Dave Smith, with his cultured left foot, stepped up first and duly put it over the bar. He got to take it again because the referee wasn't happy first time round, but missed again. And so it continued, with all of us stuffing it up. That included me, with my head still scrambled after what had happened to Ronnie earlier in the game.

We trudged back to the dressing room, totally deflated. Then John Fairgrieve, one of the travelling press pack, came in waving the rule book. We had been right, the referee was most definitely wrong. A Uefa representative from the stand was on the case by that point and pretty quickly the result of the shoot-out was overturned and we were going through. By that time, the usual adrenalin rush you get post-match had well and truly subsided, especially since we were all shattered from playing extra-time, so there were no wild scenes in the dressing room. We were glad to be through but more relieved to have the ordeal of Lisbon behind us than anything else.

The European competitions had a long winter break, so after playing in Portugal at the start of November 1971, we had to wait until 8 March the following year for the first leg of the quarter-final against Torino in Italy.

They were giants of the Italian game and the bulk of the team we met went on to win Serie A just a few years later. Torino were playing in Europe after beating AC Milan in the final of the Copa Italia the previous season and I recall their manager was headhunted by Milan soon after we faced them.

The four-month gap between the second round and the quarter-final allowed us plenty of time to get ready and the manager came up with a typically comprehensive battle plan. We had a good opportunity to get a feel for the surroundings, arriving in Italy early, even taking the chance to watch Juventus play Wolves the night before our own tie, and there was a nice and relaxed feel to the whole trip. We stayed at a brand new hotel in Asti, the home of Asti Spumante wine. It was a good half-hour drive from Turin and the hotel was still being finished, but it followed the trend of taking us away from the busy city centres and into the country. That was something that served us well in Barcelona when we reached the final.

The night before our tie, we were ferried into Turin to watch Wolves tackle Juventus in the Uefa Cup. It killed some time but also gave us a great feel for the atmosphere inside the Municipal Stadium, where both of the city's clubs played their matches, and the hostility we could expect from the home fans.

I had mixed memories of playing Italian sides from my time with Hibs, having been roundly beaten away by Napoli before getting the better of them at Easter Road. I knew how hard and cynical they could be in defence and how dangerous they were going forward – it's the same mix their club teams and national side have always relied on.

The first leg was a hard, hard game. We did well to come away with a point despite opening the scoring early, with Willie Johnston's strike in the 1–1 draw providing us with a potentially important away goal. By then, we were well versed in Waddell's system, which included using Tommy McLean more as an orthodox right midfielder than a right winger in the traditional sense. Rangers always had wingers who would go past their man, the likes of Alex Scott and Willie Henderson, but Tam had a different brief. He'd been asked to get balls in early, there was no need to get to the byline, and it was another piece of the manager's jigsaw. He also used Colin Jackson and Derek John- stone as twin centre-halves in front of Dave Smith in Turin to frustrate the home team, something totally unheard-of.

At the time, we were aware we were doing things differently the whole sweeper system, the way Bud and I were playing up front and the change in emphasis for the wingers, but it's only now that you realise how far ahead of his time Waddell was. Here was a man who a couple of years earlier had been nothing more than a newspaper columnist, yet he was out-thinking the best in Europe.

Towards the end of the first-leg, the Torino players began to throw their weight about on and off the ball, with a few punches being landed as the clock ran down. It was worse at Ibrox in the return leg, when I was being man marked by a wily old centre-half who didn't allow me an inch. We were chasing one ball over the top, shoulder-to-shoulder, when he threw out an elbow and caught me flush in the Adam's apple. I was poleaxed, and he just walked off with an air of satisfaction. They could be brutal and I suppose that's part of the reason for the success the Italians have enjoyed over the years.

There were more than 75,000 inside Ibrox for the second leg and there was a real sense that expectation was building. We'd believed from the start that we could win the competition and by then the supporters could see we meant business.

They had to be patient, though, and against Torino it took until after the break to score the winner. Alex MacDonald tucked away a Tommy McLean cross at the back post and we were on the home straight, closing in on the semi-finals.

With Bayern Munich still in the competition, we could take nothing for granted, but confidence was soaring. We'd beaten some of the best teams from France, Portugal and Italy and there was nothing to frighten us in the last four.

We all expected to be drawn against the Germans in the semi-finals and that was the way it panned out. Again, we had to travel for the first-leg and that played into our hands – no matter what the score was in the first leg, we would be confident at home against any team. Knowing exactly what we needed from the Ibrox match was ideal.

Munich played at the Grünwalder Stadion then, waiting for the Olympic Stadium to be completed. Unlike their current home, it was a compact set-up, with a capacity of 44,000 and the feeling that you could reach out and touch the fans.

More than half of the Bayern team played for Germany. Right through the core of the side they had quality from Sepp Maier in goal and Franz Beckenbauer and Hans-Georg Schwarzenbeck in defence through to Paul Breitner, Franz Roth, Uli Hoeness and Gerd Muller. Germany won the European Championships just months after we beat Bayern, and that more than anything shows what we were up against over those two ties.

They battered us in the first-half of the game in Munich. We couldn't get out from our own box as wave after wave of attacks came flooding towards our goal. To our credit, we withstood that tide in the main, with only Breitner's goal separating us when the referee blew for half-time, and in the second-half we regrouped and started to ask questions of Bayern.

Willie Mathieson, who'd been pegged inside his own six-yard box before the break, was starting to find some joy breaking forward down the left wing and our pressure paid off just a couple of minutes after the restart. I found myself one-on-one with Maier inside the box and took it past him before hammering the ball towards goal. Rainer Zobel stuck out a leg and turned it into his own net, but it would have been a goal with or without his intervention. The records show I scored five in the European run, but I always consider it to be six – like all good strikers, I'd claim for anything and that goal in Munich was mine.

A very unusual thing happened to me that night, a complete one-off. Willie Waddell, a man with an almost permanent poker face, dropped his guard and paid me a compliment. It was so unique I can still hear the words ringing in my ears. 'You did well out there tonight,' he said. Coming from Waddell, that was akin to being given a knighthood. He said it while he carried me from the park at full-time, as I'd gone down with cramp after knocking my pan in for the whole game chasing Bayern defenders down. The fact that he even helped me off the park was praise in itself; in all honesty I expected him to tell me to get up on my feet, get off the park and stop moaning.

With another 1–1 result on the road, we could look forward to Bayern coming to Glasgow in a fortnight with a lot of optimism. The game in Germany was always going to be the crucial one and we went into it with the feeling that if we could stay within a goal of them in the first leg then we'd have a great chance at Ibrox. To be playing them on home soil with the tie still level and with the benefit of an away goal was even better.

I have never witnessed anything like the scenes at Ibrox that night. The ground was heaving, the terraces looked as though they were swaying because you couldn't pick out individual faces, it was just a wall of red, white and blue, moving in time to the singing. I always smile to myself when I see the official attendance figure as 80,000 for the Bayern game – I wouldn't be surprised if it was far closer to six-figures.

I've given Willie Waddell a lot of credit for being shrewd, but when it came to the Bayern game he was also brave. John Greig sat it out through injury and that left the boss with big decisions to make. He didn't shirk them, and pulled a rabbit out of the hat when he plumped for Derek Parlane to take Greigy's place. Derek was just a young boy, 18 years of age, and had all of two first-team games under his belt.

He'd played against Clyde and Dundee, at Shawfield and Dens Park respectively, and there he was lining up against the superstars of German football in front of a packed Ibrox with the type of atmosphere none of us had ever experienced before.

Derek Johnstone was in the side too, but there was method in Waddell's thinking. Both DJ and Parlane were strong and physical, so there was no question of being out-muscled, and our training at Gullane had equipped us to outrun the Germans, as we proved with the second-half performance in Munich. The two youngsters could hold their own physically, so the only concern would be in terms of ability, and both had that in spades. With the energy of youth and the fearlessness they both had, we had an edge.

Within a minute, we were in dreamland. We attacked from the start and the visitors hardly had a touch before Sandy Jardine cut inside and curled a lovely left-foot shot past Sepp Maier. I've heard some describe it as a sclaff, but it was a beauty.

That really rattled Bayern and before long they were bickering with us and with each other. When the second goal went in, after just 22 minutes, they were well and truly beaten. That goal was straight off the training ground, a corner-kick routine Willie Johnston and I worked on. I positioned myself right on the toes of Sepp Maier, between him and the front post, to give Bud a clear target to aim for. When the ball was swung in, I went up with the big keeper and blocked him. The ball fell to Derek Parlane, who knocked it in. It wasn't a bad way for Derek to introduce himself to the Ibrox crowd.

Maier may have had a fierce reputation across the world, but he didn't have much joy that day. Our crowd were giving him pelters and at one point he dropped his pants and bared his backside at them. It wasn't the smartest of moves, they knew they were getting to him and gave him ten times as much stick for the rest of the game.

It was a momentous result for us. Bayern recovered to win the Bundesliga that season and for the next two years after that as well. They were one of the greatest sides in the world at that time and we humbled them. Across the two legs, not even the Germans could argue that we didn't deserve to go through, and with that result behind us we moved from outsiders into the position of favourites for the cup.

It was a remarkable night in Glasgow. The celebrations around Ibrox, as tens of thousands of our supporters flooded out onto the streets, were a sight to behold. You could hear it from deep within the ground.

On the same night, Celtic had gone out of the European Cup

on penalties in their semi-final at Parkhead. For the Rangers fans, Inter's win put the icing on the cake. In wider terms, the fact that two European semi-finals were played in the city on one night tells the whole story about the level football was at in Glasgow in the 1960s and 1970s. I don't think Strathclyde's finest would allow that to happen now, but it is unlikely to be a dilemma they face any time soon.

Yet back then it was almost run of the mill for Rangers and Celtic to reach the latter stages of European competitions, and 1972 was our year to shine. It was one hell of journey, but there was one more stop to go. We were heading for Barcelona.

12

Legends are born

The adrenalin was pumping, and the chants from the crowd were ringing out loud and clear around the ground. Sandy Jardine launched into a challenge on the right, sending his Russian opponent sprawling to the turf. We all waited for the referee's whistle, but it was silent, play on. The ball slid back to Dave Smith on the halfway line. I'd been standing with my back to goal, but as soon as he pulled his left leg back, I was away, turning on my heels and bearing down on the Dynamo Moscow goal, anticipating another of the quick breaks we had used to such good effect in the European Cup-Winners' Cup that season. Sure enough, a perfectly flighted through ball arrowed its way through the Spanish sky under the bright lights of the Camp Nou.

It felt like slow motion as the ball dropped over my shoulder, between the two defenders who had been like shadows to me for the first quarter of the final that night in Barcelona, and in an instant the chance was there. It took one bounce off the manicured turf, skipping past the first of my markers, and sat up in front of me. I could feel the breath of the second centre-half on my neck and see the whites of the eyes of the Dynamo goalkeeper as I lined up the shot and then bang, everything burst back into real time and a half-volley rocketed off my right boot and flew into the top right-hand corner. As soon as leather met leather, I knew there was only one place the ball was going to end up and before I had even seen it hit the back of the net, I'd wheeled round in celebration, arms aloft and roaring with joy.

The noise was deafening as the cheers went up around the vast stadium and all of a sudden we had one hand on the cup. It is the moment that has come to define my career, the first goal of the final, which set us on our way to the 3–2 win against the Russians that ended the long wait for a European prize to find its way to the Ibrox trophy room. To play a part in that success, let alone score, is a source of enormous satisfaction. Even now, close to four decades later, I can replay the occasion second by second. In fact, as time passes the gravity of what we did that night grows. I'm proud to say I was part of that team and of that achievement. It was a remarkable occasion to cap a wonderful season and all of us who were wrapped up in the event cherish our memories of 24 May 1972.

That was the date all of our great hopes and ambitions came true, but the final was about more than just 90 minutes of football. From the moment we qualified by beating Bayern Munich, the prospect of lifting the trophy in Barcelona enveloped us. There were 35 days between that win against Bayern and the match against Dynamo Moscow and it felt like a lifetime. If we could have played the final the next day we would have gladly done it.

Instead we had to pace ourselves, going through the motions back home, when all we wanted to do was get on the plane. In hindsight, the build-up was surreal. At the time we thought nothing of it. As we geared up for the match of our lives, we were sent out to face Highland League opposition in bounce games to keep us sharp. It sounds utterly crazy to be playing friendlies against non-league part-timers at such a vital stage, but we trusted Willie Waddell implicitly and none of us so much as raised an eyebrow as we ran out against the boys from the north in our final warm-up matches before departing for the continent. We rounded off with a bounce game against St Mirren and everything was falling nicely into place.

Waddell and his coaching staff knew our team inside out.

Young gun. In full flight at Easter Road wearing Hibs colours with pride. It was in Leith that my career took off. *Courtesy of Eric McCowat*

Perfect match. Linda and I toast our engagement in 1968.

Above. Lip service. Bobby Duncan (right) and me during our time together on the Easter Road staff. It was Bobby who gave me the Louis The Lip nickname that has followed me to this day.

Right. Power play. Golf became one of my great passions after becoming a full-time footballer. This is me on the tee at Gleneagles.

Above. Ibrox calling. Putting pen to paper for Rangers following contract talks in Edinburgh as Matt Taylor and manager Davie White look on.

Left. Blue heaven. I got my hands on the famous jersey in 1968.

Above. Life through a lens. After becoming Scotland's first £100,000 player I had to grow used to the media attention that followed me on and off the park.

Right. Hero to villain. This is me in action against my old side Hibs, tangling with John Blackley. I scored a hat-trick in my first match against my former team-mates. *Courtesy of Eric McCowat*

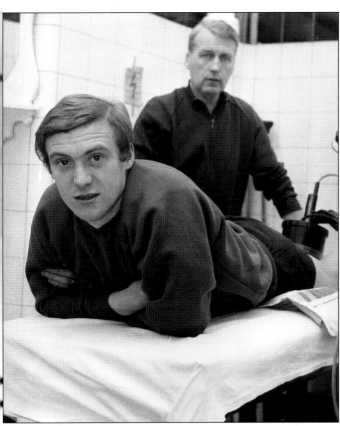

Left. In safe hands. The attention to detail at Rangers on and off the park was second to none. This is me being looked after by trainer Davie Kinnear.

Below. Action men. Ronnie McKinnon and I run out for another game as Rangers team-mates. Ronnie and I became great friends and went through a lot of highs and lows together at Ibrox.

Above. Keeping pace. That's me, wearing my No.2 training kit, on the heels of Dave Smith and John Greig during one of the infamous Jock Wallace sessions at Ibrox.

Right. Living the dream. Nothing could ever match the thrill of scoring goals for Rangers.
Courtesy of Eric McCowat

Left. Making history. Leading the line with Alan Gilzean during our 8–0 win over Cyprus at Hampden in 1969. My four goals in that game have yet to be matched by a Scotland player. *Courtesy of Eric McCowat*

Below. No escape. Even on honeymoon in Majorca there was time for football. That's me on the far left along with Davie White (far right), who checked into the hotel where Linda and I were spending our honeymoon.

Left. Star quality. Checking my score card with American golf legend Billy Casper during the Sean Connery Pro-Am in 1970.

Below. From joy to sorrow. As I celebrated this equaliser against Celtic on 2 January 1971 I had no idea of the disaster which was unfolding at Ibrox. The tragic events of that day will never leave me. *Courtesy of Eric McCowat*

Captain's influence. I developed an enormous respect for John Greig during our time together at Rangers. He had to display all his leadership qualities in the aftermath of the disaster.

On our way to Barca. My goal from Andy Penman's free-kick against Sporting Lisbon at Ibrox.
Courtesy of Eric McCowat

Right. Reason to be cheerful. That's me with my hand on the prize at long last, soaking up the feeling of being a winner in Europe post-match at the Nou Camp along with Peter McCloy, Jim Denny, Dave Smith, Derek Johnstone, Andy Penman, Gerry Neef, Alex MacDonald and Alfie Conn.

Above. They think it's all over. I've never run as fast as I did at full-time in Barcelona, heading for the calm of the dressing room as the joyous Rangers fans had their celebrations ruined by the Spanish police.
Courtesy of Eric McCowat

Right. Career highlight. Winning at Camp Nou was the biggest achievement of my football career. *Courtesy of Eric McCowat*

Left. The morning after the night before. Together with John Greig and Willie Johnston I celebrate the European Cup Winners' Cup win at our Barcelona hotel.

Below. Flying high. Linda and I celebrate the team's European success with Willie Johnston and his wife Margaret on the plane back from Barcelona.

The winning team. Standing shoulder to shoulder with Jock Wallace in the back row, this is me with the 1972 team parading the trophy back on Scottish soil. *Courtesy of Eric McCowat*

Sent to Coventry. I took many happy memories from my time in Coventry City colours.

Left. Gunning for the Gunners. Arsenal defender Jeff Blockley, a former Coventry favourite, keeps a close eye on me during a First Division match during my City days.

Below. Full focus. This is me enjoying a spot of rest and relaxation on the bowling green during the Rangers tour of Australia in 1975.

Happy in hoops. Moving to Kilmarnock on loan gave me the chance to play regular first team football again. This is me, in the blue and white hoops of Killie, scoring for my new side.

Keep smiling. I always tried to play the game with a smile on my face, and when the enjoyment faded I decided it was time to hang up my boots once and for all. *Courtesy of Eric McCowat*

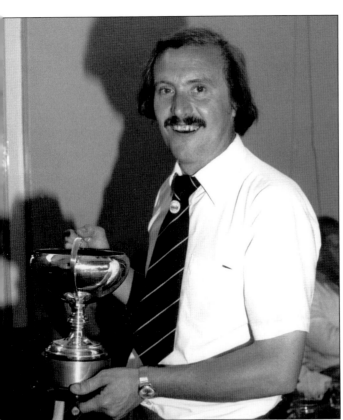

Left. From blue to green. Bowling has given me my fix of competitive sport since retiring from football. This picture is from one of my wins with Linlithgow Bowling Club in the 1980s.

Below. Fame at last. Willie Johnston and I mark our induction to the Rangers Hall of Fame.

Together again. The Barca Bears on the pitch at Ibrox to celebrate the 30th anniversary of our triumph in 1972.

The winning team. My grandchildren Ethan, Cole, Emma and Jack are the apple of my eye.

They had us in the best physical shape of our lives, but understood that all the training in the world is no substitute for game time. They made sure we were finely tuned and the Highland challenges were part of the master plan.

On top of their part in keeping us fit, those fixtures also served as a handy distraction for a group of players who were chomping at the bit. You might think there would be enough to keep us occupied while preparing for a major final, but everything was done for us – all we had to do was turn up for the coach to the airport on time. Even the wives and girlfriends were taken care of, joining us for the trip as part of a deal that had been struck earlier in the campaign. They hadn't accompanied the official party for any of the earlier ties but the manager, keen to build up the sense of importance and occasion, decided the routine should be changed for the final. The one condition was that our better halves would not be joining us at the team hotel, instead they were installed by the club on the other side of Barcelona in a hotel at Sitges. Linda was more nervous than I was as we boarded the flight, she knew just what it meant to me to come back with a winner's medal.

The wives and girlfriends were part of the official party, but like everyone else I had friends and family travelling any way they could, joining the massed ranks of Rangers supporters who arrived in the city by boat, plane, train, bus and car. I was at a recent game between Falkirk and Rangers at Falkirk Stadium when a supporter approached me and showed me his boarding card, match ticket and other travel passes for the final in Barcelona. It wasn't just a short hop for these guys, it took weeks of planning to organise the trips, not to mention months of saving to foot the bill.

For us it was far simpler. We were treated like kings throughout our stay, made to feel special and well aware that nothing was being left to chance. We flew out from Prestwick on the Sunday before the final and were taken by coach from the airport on the outskirts of Barcelona to our hotel in the Catalan countryside. The Gran Hotel Rey Don Jaime was the perfect base, tucked away from the hubbub of the city centre and the supporters who flocked to Spain for the match. There was nothing to bother us, all we had to do was train, rest and eat well. The hotel wasn't grand in scale, but it had everything we needed. There was time to relax by the pool, although for most of the time we were wrapped up in thick tracksuits, protected from the Mediterranean sunshine on the orders of a manager who was concerned that he might lose half his team to sunburn. He even made the sprint coach, Tom Paterson, guard the hotel corridors to ensure nobody could disturb our afternoon siestas, which were all carefully timetabled.

Most of our preparation was done before we even set foot on Spanish soil, so our time in Barcelona was spent mainly at the hotel. We did a few light training sessions, including an opportunity to try out the Camp Nou for size, but nothing more than that. In truth, it was a drag because we wanted to get out and play, but the spirit in the camp helped us pass the time.

Willie Waddell had watched the Russians in action, although access to their games was difficult and footage of their league was non-existent. Dynamo's draw in Europe that season didn't exactly help, since they played teams from outside the mainstream all the way through to the final.

They squeezed past Olympiakos from Greece in the first round and then the Turkish side Eskisehirspor. In the quarter-finals, they overcame Red Star Belgrade and needed penalties to pass Dynamo Berlin in the semi-final. Although none of the Eastern Bloc sides were ever soft touches, it's fair to say that we would have had an easier time playing Red Star and Berlin than we did against Torino and Bayern in our last couple of ties. Moscow enjoyed the easier route to the final and that gave us confidence, most people had us marked down as favourites before a ball was kicked.

Despite the obvious difficulty of uncovering information about the Russian players, the manager still did his usual job of tracking down pictures and details of each member of their squad. We were left in no doubt that we could not be complacent; after all, Dynamo were one of the major teams in the Russian game. Any side that can count Lev Yashin as one of its most prominent former players has to be taken seriously. They had never played outside the top tier of their domestic game and still haven't, as far as I'm aware.

Willie Waddell was convinced that if we prevented their captain Josef Szabo from being an influence then we would stop their team, so John Greig was detailed early in the preparations to take care of him. He wasn't told to take the player out of the game, but Waddell wanted Greigy to make his presence felt early on. Other than that specific role, the rest of us were to carry on doing what we had done in the previous rounds.

Although we didn't know our final team until the day of the game, we had a good idea. Most of the places filled themselves, the only exception was one berth in midfield where there were three players vying for it: Alfie Conn, Andy Penman and Derek Johnstone.

Each had their own merits and probably all three had prepared themselves for the pain of missing out. Alfie and Derek were young and fearless, both capable of playing in the middle of the park and bossing a game in their own way, while Andy was the wise old head who could hurt teams with his wicked crosses and thundrous shots. None of us could even begin to second guess which way Willie Waddell would go.

The now infamous training-ground injury to Colin Jackson on the eve of the game eased the selection problem slightly, although Waddell would far rather have had the headache of choosing one from three than having to replace Bomber. When he went down in training in Barcelona, I don't think any of us had an inkling how serious it was or that he would miss the final.

Colin was a tough guy and was obviously in pain, having done his ankle, but you never really expect the worst. Unfortunately for him, he had to sit out what would have been the biggest game of his career. It was devastating for the big man. Of course it was the same for Ronnie McKinnon, who was still nursing his broken leg, but at least Ron was prepared for it.

I have a feeling the manager would have found room for Derek Johnstone even if Colin had been fit, but the late injury guaranteed DJ his place. With his ability in the air and timing in the tackle, Derek was a like-for-like replacement.

That just left only one choice to make: either Andy Penman or Alfie Conn. When the team announcement was made it was young Alfie who got the nod. Andy was an easygoing type of character and if it hurt him he never let it show, typical of the great professional that he was.

That was how the line-up of McCloy, Jardine, Mathieson, Greig, Johnstone, Smith, McLean, Conn, Stein, MacDonald and Johnston came to be. Now we knew, all that was left to do was count down to kick-off. There was a pre-match meal at the hotel before we boarded the coach for the Camp Nou.

It was a Wednesday night and I'll never forget how deadly quiet the streets of Barcelona were as the bus snaked its way into the city. We hardly saw a soul until we turned a corner and were hit by a wall of red, white and blue. There were Rangers supporters swarming around us as we made the final approach to the ground, banging on the windows and cheering us on. The coach was reduced to no more than walking pace and just moving through the crowd to the front door of the stadium was a battle.

We had time for the traditional walk onto the park before we got changed. The Camp Nou's unique in the way that you have to climb stairs from the tunnel up to ground level, so the first thing you see as your head pops into the open air is the pitch, not the 100,000 capacity stadium towering over you. It was the grass and not the terracing that caught my eye, compared to the tired old end-of-season parks we'd been playing on back home it was perfectly suited to the way we liked to zip the ball about.

There's always been a misconception about that period in the Scottish game that Celtic had the silk and Rangers had the steel. That was unfair on us because we had players right through the team who liked to get the ball down and pass it. The Camp Nou was as good a stage as any to show the world.

We lined up before kick-off and all around us there were Rangers supporters, in fact you couldn't even make out a single Russian in the crowd. That was one of the quirks of playing a team from the East in those days, when there wasn't the freedom of movement there is now. It made for an odd atmosphere, with our every move greeted by roars from the 30,000 or so blues in Barcelona and any attack from Moscow bringing silence.

To be fair, our fans had plenty to shout about in the first half. If you watch the highlights the first thing you see is Josef Szabo, the Dynamo danger man, being absolutely melted by John Greig. Team orders were carried out to the letter. The game was just seconds old when Mr Szabo felt the full force of the skipper. We had a Spanish referee that night and he turned out to be a bit more tolerant than his countrymen in the police force, letting Greigy off without so much as a warning. A few more challenges in the same mould soon quietened Szabo down and we didn't see much of him as an attacking force at all.

Instead, it was us who asked most of the questions and when I scored the opening goal after 25 minutes we were well and truly in the ascendancy. The goal brought the crowd flooding onto the pitch and it took a couple of minutes for it all to calm down again, a sign of things to come. There was no malice in the pitch invasion, it was just a culmination of the excitement that had built up over the long wait for the game. They'd come a long way to savour the occasion and were going all out to enjoy it.

When Willie Johnston made it 2–0 five minutes before half-time, there was a sense of relief as much as joy. With a one-goal lead you always feel vulnerable, but with a two-goal cushion you can relax, particularly with a team as well organised and drilled as ours. That goal from Bud was a perfect example of how good he was with his head, helped no end by the quality of the ball whipped in from the right by Dave Smith.

We went in at half-time with the adrenalin flowing and not even the manager, who would normally err on the side of caution, could see a way back for them. He wanted us to keep doing the things we had done in the first-half and go for further goals to finish it off once and for all. We were by far the superior team and when you are involved in a game like that, you find everyone wants to get on the ball and play, you feel the confidence growing.

When it moved to 3–0 after the break, we thought we were on easy street. Peter McCloy's long kick-out came booming towards me, I didn't get a touch but both centre-halves had come to meet me and when it bounced clear of us, all that was left for Bud to do was to run in and score. He kept his cool and finished with the type of composure we'd come to expect of him. A lot of people tried to argue that he was offside, but that's only because he'd timed his run so well, checking it perfectly to hold the line just long enough to stay onside.

I was pretty confident that there were more goals in the game for us and with my tail up, I was on the prowl for at least another one to match Willie's double.

There was certainly no conscious decision to sit back and defend our lead, and no word from the touchline either. Yet we found ourselves on the back foot after Dynamo pulled it back to 3–1 through Vladimir Estrekov's goal. To their eternal credit, the Russians kept going to the very last. We must have been the fittest team in Europe at that time, but they stuck with us every step of the way.

Their second goal, just a couple of minutes from full-time,

really put us on edge. There was a whistle for a free-kick that we all thought signalled the end, we thought we'd done it. So did the supporters and that was when they started spilling onto the park again. Obviously it wasn't over yet and the fans were herded off the pitch. When it really was all over, the invasion started again, far bigger than those previously and generating panic among the Spanish police. Had they left the supporters to make their own way back onto the terraces, there would have been no problem, let them get their piece of turf or whatever souvenir they wanted and allow matters to run their course. Instead, they opted for conflict and it proved to be the wrong choice.

I didn't hang around to see the outcome, I legged it as fast as I could back to the dressing room. It's the only time I've ever beaten Willie Johnston in a race. I turned to him when he came haring into the dressing room after me and just said, 'What kept you?' I was first back in, with players trooping in one-by-one in different states. Some lost boots and other bits of kit and poor John Greig was in agony after one of the fans jumped on his injured foot during the celebrations.

We'd all seen the pandemonium up above on ground level, but it wasn't a concern for us. We were celebrating just as much as the fans, the dressing room was full of noise and we were practically bouncing off the walls with joy. The first I was aware that things weren't going to plan outside was when Willie Waddell called John Greig aside and word soon spread through the team that we weren't going to get our lap of honour or trophy presentation.

Instead, John went away to collect it in a back room and brought it through to us while we were enjoying a few Spanish beers in the big bath in the centre of the Camp Nou dressing room. The cup was soon filled up and the party started properly once we had that trophy safely in our grasp.

Jock Wallace followed behind John and handed out a medal

to each of us. It's not a big medal, but a distinctive one, a gold rectangle that's different from anything else I've ever seen in football. Barely seconds after we had been given the medals, Jock came back round all of the boys asking for them back so the club could get them engraved for us. I wasn't keen on it. I'd just knocked my pan in for a season to get the medal, blood, sweat and tears had been spilled on the European run, so the thought of handing it back wasn't too appealing. Jock was adamant, though, and we had a few choice words to say to each other before I eventually relented and handed it back. I found over the years that with Jock it was a losing battle trying to win an argument but it never stopped me from trying.

By the time the party in the dressing room died down and we returned to the bus, there was little sign of the problems there had been with the crowd after the final whistle. We obviously knew there had been a pitch invasion after being caught up in it, but I'd seen that happen plenty of times before without any problems in clearing the crowd quickly.

It wasn't until we got back to the team hotel and met up with our wives that we realised the true extent of what had gone on. They had seen it all from their seats in the stand and not surprisingly it had shaken them, particularly the ferocity with which the Spanish police set about the Rangers fans. It was a big relief that our friends and family avoided the worst of the trouble on the night and although it was impossible not to be distracted by what had unfolded, we tried not to let it spoil the occasion. It was a phenomenal achievement and it deserved to be remembered for the right reasons.

We had a cracking night at the hotel, with good food and drink flowing freely, before the wives and girlfriends returned to their base. After that, the party carried on well into the next morning, I don't think anyone wanted it to end. It had to, of course, and there were a few fragile bodies on the flight back to Prestwick.

We were ushered straight through to the plane on the tarmac at Barcelona, the authorities obviously still worried about the potential for a crowd surge if the fans caught sight of us in the terminal building. We were cheered from afar as we climbed the steps to the plane and the scale of the achievement was slowly beginning to sink in by then.

There were swarms of photographers waiting for us when we touched down on Scottish soil and a television crew joined us on the bus from the airport back to the ground. The great Arthur Montford had just finished interviewing John Greig about the joy of making up for the disappointment of losing in the 1967 European final when he turned to me and asked, 'Colin, which of your goals was the best?' I looked at him deadpan and said, 'Arthur, I only scored one.' The bus erupted and I swear his face turned as bright as one of his famous jackets. He's never forgotten it, either. I met him years later when I was inducted into the Ibrox hall of fame and when I went up to the stage to collect the award, he took one look at me and said, 'Don't mention it.'

Our next official duty was to parade the trophy around Ibrox. It sounds like a grand idea until you factor in that it was pouring with rain and we were on the back of an old flatbed lorry rather than an open-top bus. Still, none of that mattered to us or the tens of thousands of supporters who turned out.

It could have been blowing blizzards and I don't think it would have taken the edge off the celebrations in the blue half of Glasgow that day and for weeks after. It was our time to enjoy the spotlight and we did just that.

13

The Barca Bears and me

The spirit within the squad that took us all the way to the Camp Nou was second to none. We played hard, worked hard and also knew how to enjoy ourselves at the right time. If ever there was a team that defined the all-for-one-and-one-for-all mentality, this was it. We shared some amazing times and came away from that season with memories that will never leave us.

Because of that togetherness, there's a popular misconception that we have all lived in each other's pockets in the years since Barcelona, but nothing could be further from the truth. Pretty soon after, we began to go our separate ways and while our paths crossed again in the years that followed, it is never the same as when you are sharing a dressing room and grafting together on the training pitch.

Fortunately, we are brought back together for reunions frequently and when the crew is back together again, the years soon roll back. It is all too easy to forget that we're a bit longer in the tooth now, because we revert to type when the group's in place. The jokers are still making wisecracks, the loud ones are just as vocal and the calming influences are still doing their best to keep everyone in check.

In hindsight, it is easy to see that there was a great mix of personalities and players in that squad. Knowing Willie Waddell as I do, I don't think the make-up of the team was any accident. He looked at character just as much as he studied a player's ability, and that's a big part of being a successful manager. He brought together a team that clicked, on and off the park.

Outside Ibrox there were differing levels of recognition for the Barca Bears. It was a travesty that Peter McCloy never won more caps than he did. Peter was the consummate athlete, nobody at Ibrox could touch him when he got into his stride, and he was a really good shot stopper. His only downfall was that he was just too damn nice. If he'd been more dominant, been willing to knock a few more people out of his way, he would have played far more games for Scotland. Often at training, I'd give him a dig as we waited for balls to come across and he'd be annoyed at me, but you had to train the way you played. With his frame, Peter would have struck terror into the heart of any centre-forward if he'd been a bit more ruthless, but he preferred to rely on brain rather than brawn and has always been a gentle giant.

For all we seemed to have a reputation as a gritty team, we didn't have any hammer-throwers. Sandy Jardine was a case in point, a defender by trade, but tackling was never his strong suit. Sandy was far better with the ball at his feet and starting attacks, always looking to play a pass. He started life playing further forward and not long before I arrived he was regularly playing as a striker, filling in after the Berwick Rangers cup defeat had brought the careers of George McLean and Jim Forrest to a premature end.

Willie Mathieson was the opposite, he would tackle all day long and once he got the bit between his teeth, he just wouldn't let go. I've been on the receiving end of a few of Willie's challenges in training and when you were hit by one of them, you knew all about it. He was always 100 per cent fair though, hard but not dirty. He had much more to his game than tackling, though, with the energy to get up and down the park and join in the attacks, a hugely underrated member of the team.

John Greig didn't have to worry about slipping under the radar though, he was very much the figurehead and, in many ways, still is. He wasn't the greatest player in the world but as a captain he was superb and I have enormous respect for the way he went about his job. That doesn't mean we're the best of friends mind you, it was more of a working relationship. In any group of colleagues you are never going to get a collection of individuals who see eye to eye all the time, and Greigy didn't go out of his way to try to be Mr Popular. It was part and parcel of his gruff personality.

Derek Johnstone was a total contrast, he went about the game in the same way he approaches life – full of fun and energy. The game in Barcelona was huge for Derek and he passed the test with flying colours. I rate DJ very highly. I like to think I'm a decent judge of a striker and he was a real star in that respect. He had everything a good forward needs. I also had first-hand experience of how good a defender he was, having come up against him in training. It was a tough shift for a forward trying to get the better of him because in the air and on the deck he was simply superb.

Dave Smith was the perfect foil for Derek's raw energy in 1972. Dave was one of the older heads in the side by that point, one of the veterans of the 1967 European Cup-Winners' Cup final, and as composed a player as the game has ever seen. His range of passing was a joy to watch. Dave's one of the best footballers I've ever played against, as I did when I was with Hibs and then in training after going to Ibrox. He wasn't the fastest in a straight sprint, but he always seemed to have a yard on you because he was one step ahead in his mind. His hidden talent was table tennis, with the two of us have some real humdingers of games between training sessions over the years.

Tommy McLean was another one of the great thinkers in the team. He was a very astute winger and there was always logic in the runs he made and passes he played. A lot of wingers will beat a man or make a run for the sake of it, but not Tommy. He had a great variety to his play; if the run to the byline was on he'd make it, but if it made more sense to cross early then he was just as happy to do that and the quality of his balls into the box were excellent. He always had a very analytical mind, so it was no surprise when he moved into management.

In many ways Alfie Conn was the total opposite, he played off the cuff. It is easy to forget that Alfie was just a young pup when he played in Barcelona. He'd been around for a couple of years and nothing fazed him. He had the ability to go out and do his thing regardless of who he was playing against or what the surroundings were. His whole game was based on the confidence he had in his own ability, and that confidence was totally justified.

Alfie put in a heck of a shift against Moscow that night and Alex MacDonald, beside him in midfield, was another who ran himself into the ground. Alex had amazing energy and wore his heart on his sleeve. But there was much more to his game than getting around the park and winning possession, he was cute with the ball and also made brilliant runs past the front players into the box. That brought him his share of goals and if you have somebody like Doddie behind you chipping in like that, it eases the pressure. It also gives defenders an awful lot to think about, and that helps open things up nicely.

What I will never understand for as long as I live is how Alex went through his entire career without winning a Scotland cap. He played with distinction for Rangers, winning trophy after trophy at home and abroad, and was such a vital player for a succession of managers at club level. Yet not a single Scotland manager saw fit to play Doddie, one of the game's biggest injustices as far as I'm concerned. I don't know why his face didn't fit at Hampden, but he would never have let anyone down.

Not that playing for Scotland is always a bed of roses, of course, as Willie Johnston would testify. Bud and I have travelled the world together representing Rangers since 1972. We were good friends then and are probably even better pals now, you could never tire of Willie's company.

He was also a joy to play alongside and a nightmare to go up against. He was as quick with the ball as he was in a straight sprint and so switched on that he simply terrified defenders. He could mix it, too, when he had to, and that bit of devilment made him the star he was. Okay, he found himself on the wrong side of the authorities more than he would have liked, but if you'd taken the edge off Bud's game you would have been left with half the player.

Like so many of the players in that team he wasn't the biggest, but he made up for it in personality and determination. Tommy McLean, Alfie Conn and Alex MacDonald were hardly giants, and it makes me laugh when I hear people say that we were a defensive side and the Lisbon Lions were the football playing team of the era.

If that had been the game plan, the boss would have packed the side with 6ft muscle men, not little ball players like we had. Even the defence wasn't particularly negative, with Jardine and Smith happier going forward than tackling and DJ a proven striker in his own right. Mathieson liked to bomb forward, too, so there was no question of us being a defensive outfit.

By the time we got onto the pitch in Barcelona two of our best defenders were missing, because of the injuries to Colin Jackson and Ronnie McKinnon. Bomber Jackson was horrible to play against for any centre-forward, so strong in the air and a tenacious tackler. He loved to defend and every team needs a player in that mould.

Ronnie's biggest asset was his pace, which you had to see up close to fully appreciate. He didn't always need it, since he had such a good football brain, but that type of pace is a godsend if you are under threat. There was much more to Ron's game than that, though, he was an inspirational defender. It was a travesty that his career was cut short.

Willie Henderson's time at Rangers was curtailed in different circumstances, but we still missed him after the manager decided to let him leave during the run to the final. It goes without saying that Willie was a brilliant talent, but he was also the social convenor. If there was an excuse for a party, he would find it and get it organised. Willie makes a living now recounting the tales from his playing days, but he was just as good a storyteller back then. He lived his life to the full, there's no doubt about that.

Younger players like Graham Fyfe, Derek Parlane and Jim Denny played their part, too, and Alex Miller was in and around the squad by then, but none expected in their heart of hearts to play in the final, unlike Andy Penman.

In many ways, Andy was the unluckiest of all. In contrast to Ron and Colin, he was fit and ready to play his part but didn't make the cut. Andy was in his 30s at the time of the final and one of the father-figures to the younger players in the squad. Perhaps due to the diabetes he was eventually diagnosed with, Andy was no marathon runner, but with the way he played the game he didn't need to be, It was effortless for him and he could carve teams open. He also had one of the most powerful shots I have ever seen. In training, I'd often go in goals to give Peter McCloy and the other keepers a break, and when Andy hit a shot in your direction it stayed hit. He didn't just sting your palms, he almost took your hand clean off. As a league winner with Dundee, his best days were probably at Dens but it was a pleasure to play in the same team as him.

Andy's death in 1994 shattered the illusion that we are all invincible. He was far too young to die, but nobody knows what is around the corner. For that reason as much as any, it makes the time the remaining Barca Bears spend together even more valuable. I'm proud to say that it is still all for one and one for all, just as it was all those years ago.

14

Sent to Coventry

It can take just a few seconds to turn your life upside down, as I discovered to my cost in the wake of our success in Barcelona. I came back from Spain feeling invincible, believing that the win in Europe was just the start of great things for the team Willie Waddell had assembled.

Little did I realise that I would be one of the first to leave as the manager set about demolishing the victorious team and rebuilding almost from scratch. Although Waddell handed over day-to-day control to Jock Wallace after Barcelona, there's no doubt in my mind that he still had a massive influence when it came to which players came and went. That was particularly true in the immediate aftermath of the 1972 win, and while the record books show that it was Jock who sold me, I've always known that it was Willie Waddell who engineered it.

The speed and brutality with which the team was picked apart was frightening. Willie Johnston was the first to go, heading off to West Brom, while Alfie Conn and myself were not far behind. Dave Smith lasted another season after us, and Willie Mathieson was another one moved on relatively swiftly.

Within two years of winning the European Cup-Winners' Cup, half the team had been sold for a big profit or allowed to move on to pastures new. At the time I thought they had got it all wrong but if you look at the success the club enjoyed in the following years it is difficult to argue with the way they went about their business. The policy of ripping the team apart would prove to be either brave or foolish and, even although I was one of the victims, I'm honest enough to say it was the former.

There were different reasons for disposing of each player. In my case, it appeared to be a case of punishing me for a crime I simply didn't commit. The beginning of the end was at the start of the 1972/73 season. I'd come back from the summer holidays with a spring in my step and desperate to get going again, but that enthusiasm was soon nipped in the bud.

I was sitting in the dressing room after training one day when the message was sent down that I had to report to the manager's office. The room was at the top of the marble staircase, fitted with a light above the door with either 'wait' or 'enter' lit up. It was always on wait because everything was on Willie Waddell's terms, right down to when you opened the door.

I had no idea what to expect, I could have been about to get a pat on the back and a pay rise for all I knew. After all, Barcelona had been a pretty comprehensive success for the team as a whole and me personally. Instead, I was hit with an accusation that I knew nothing about.

I went into the manager's office and he was in his usual place behind the big wooden desk, accompanied by Willie Thornton that day. I was asked to explain comments I had apparently made to a reporter after it was claimed on the radio that I had said that it was Colin Stein and Willie Johnston who won the European trophy, not Willie Waddell or anyone else. Waddell was absolutely furious, even although I told him I'd never said anything of the sort. That was the truth, I knew nothing about the reports and quotes attributed to me, but there was no way I was going to be allowed to explain my way out of this one.

I received a royal dressing-down and was sent back down the stairs with my tail between my legs. No more was said about it and I went back to training just the same as usual until one day I was summoned up the stairs again. This time, there were even fewer pleasantries. I sat down and Willie Waddell told me that

Coventry City had made a bid that he had accepted. He told me I was free to speak to them and I could tell from his body language that it wasn't a suggestion that I should talk to the English side, it was effectively an order. I knew there was no sense in trying to dig my heels in, because nobody won a battle with the Deedle.

I was gobsmacked, it was a real shock to the system. I had a wife and baby daughter at home and no inclination to uproot them, but it sounded very much like I had no choice in the matter. Aside from that, I was happy at Rangers, it was the club I wanted to play for and every day at work was a dream come true for me. In an instant, that was snatched away.

To this day, I don't know the whole truth behind what happened that morning. Reading between the lines, I have always thought that it must have been down to the belief that I was in some way trying to take the glory for myself and undermine the manager in the process. Maybe there was another reason, maybe it was a football choice, but it was never explained to me. I was so shocked, stunned into silence, that I didn't get the chance to demand an answer.

Certainly Jock wasn't being left short of options when I moved on. He already had Derek Johnstone able to score goals and young Derek Parlane was staking a claim for a first-team place. It was DP rather than DJ who eventually filled my boots and he did a cracking job for the club over the years.

My departure happened very quickly, so I suppose Waddell and Wallace must have had some sort of contingency plan in their minds.

I started the 1972/73 season where I expected to, in the first-team and with the No. 9 shirt on my back. We breezed through the League Cup group games and I scored a couple of goals, so everything looked as though it was going to plan. The major fly in the ointment was the European ban that was looming over us after the pitch invasion in Barcelona, but that battle was being fought in the corridors of power at Uefa, so for the players it wasn't a major concern. Obviously we wanted to defend the trophy, but we were back to focusing on the domestic competitions by the time the season began. When the First Division kicked off I was still leading the line, but by October it was all change and I was sent to Coventry. Rangers won the Scottish Cup at the end of that season but lost out on the league by a single point. I wish I had still been around to see if I could have made a difference, perhaps have helped win the one match that would have brought the title back to Ibrox, but the management had different ideas.

After being told by the club that the Coventry offer had been approved, I headed straight for Carlisle for talks with City. Gordon Milne, who ran the team under general manager Joe Mercer, met me along with the club secretary Eddie Plumley. Eddie had everything laid out in typically efficient fashion, he had a reputation as one of football's great organisers, and for good reason. In fact, he was head-hunted by Elton John to run Watford in the late 1970s, although the Coventry connection continued when his son Ian became involved in more recent times.

On the table that day was a great offer, with a substantial pay rise and plenty of other perks thrown in for good measure. That included a percentage of the £140,000 transfer fee, capped at 5 per cent by the league but topped up by a loyalty bonus that was written into the contract to compensate. Financially it was attractive, but the main reason I said yes was because I felt I had no choice in the matter.

I didn't know an awful lot about Coventry but had watched from afar as they had crept up through the leagues. They were a Fourth Division side in the late 1950s but, in the space of eight years, had risen right through the leagues into the First Division by 1967.

Jimmy Hill was a major factor in that progress, as the manager when they won the Third Division and Second Division, and his influence was all around the place even when I was there and that was a good five years after he quit to move into television. It was Jimmy who helped redevelop the ground, it was Jimmy who changed the club colours to sky blue and it was Jimmy who introduced match programmes at Highfield Road. His legacy was amazing, and impressive, too.

I agreed to join the club after that meeting with Gordon in a Carlisle hotel, even although I'd never set foot in the city, let alone visited the club. But from what Gordon told me I got a good feeling about what I was signing up for.

Coventry were firmly established as a First Division side by the early 1970s and although there had been a few brushes with relegation, they had also flirted with breaking in amongst the big boys at the top end of the league and had played in Europe just a couple of years before I arrived. Then when they brought in Joe Mercer, who had achieved tremendous success with Manchester City in winning the league, cup and European Cup-Winners' Cup, it was a signal of intent.

Joe arrived at Highfield Road in the summer of 1972 and he was given a big fat chequebook to try to repeat what he had done at Maine Road. I was the first of the major signings but not the last, and he pulled together a pretty tasty team in a short period of time. The fee was a club record for Coventry and they enjoyed splashing the cash so much that they went right out and did it again to snap up Tommy Hutchison.

The splurge was partly funded by the sale of Jeff Blockley, a big powerful defender who was a favourite at Highfield Road, at around the same time. Arsenal paid £200,000 for Jeff and all of that money was reinvested in the squad, something the chairman deserves credit for. I had some tussles with Jeff after he joined the Gunners and always found him a tough customer, even though the Arsenal fans gave him a rough ride. He'd been brought in to replace Frank McLintock and despite winning an England cap, he never lived up to expectations and was sold to Leicester within a couple of years.

It fell on Joe Mercer to replace Jeff as part of his master plan and the club couldn't have entrusted the job to a finer person. Joe was a great character, a real star of a man. He was a fine player in his day by all accounts, a legend in the eyes of supporters at Everton and Arsenal, but I knew him as a man, not a footballer and in that respect he was a legend too. Joe passed away more than 20 years ago, but I can still picture his big smile, the first thing you noticed about him when he walked into the room. Just like Davie White before him, Joe put a lot of faith in me when he and Gordon Milne took me south for a big fee. It didn't matter to him if you cost £1 or £100,000 he treated everybody the same way. I'll always remember my brother Eric dropping in to the club for a quick visit and disappearing with Joe for a blether. The two of them got on like a house on fire and I didn't see him again for hours, Joe had time for everyone and would change his own plans at the drop of a hat to make sure others were looked after.

I've never heard of anyone with a bad word to say about the man and his credentials spoke volumes. While I was at the club, he had a spell as caretaker manager with England in 1974, holding the fort after Sir Alf Ramsey stepped down, and I've often wondered how he would have fared if he had taken the job on a permanent basis. He certainly had the personality and charisma you need to be successful as an international manager.

I first met Joe when I pitched up in Coventry to complete the formalities and start work. Just like when I left Hibs for Rangers, I didn't even have time to say goodbye to my teammates. I left Ibrox for talks with Coventry and ended up not going back to Ibrox at all.

Initially, I was put up at the Leofric Hotel in the centre of Coventry, a big modern building at that time with a reputation as *the* place to stay, but my new home in the Midlands for the next nine months was to be the quieter Allesley Hotel in a nice little village on the road to Birmingham. Linda and Nicola stayed back at home in Linlithgow for the whole of my first season in England, to allow me time to settle in. I'd never been away from home turf in my life, so it was difficult being catapulted into a new city all alone and living out of a suitcase, but we got through it. I'd fit in visits home every fortnight, or more often if we were playing up in Newcastle or elsewhere in the north, and got to know the road over the border like the back of my hand. It was a fair old drive, but I was desperate to return to see my wife and daughter, so the journey passed quickly enough.

On my first trip south I was pleasantly surprised by what lay in store for me. Highfield Road wasn't the biggest ground in the world, not a patch on Ibrox in terms of size, but it was perfectly formed. It could hold somewhere in the region of 35,000 and there were a couple of new stands, complete with hospitality boxes, something even Rangers didn't have back then. The facilities put my old club to shame, in all honesty. Everything was perfectly maintained and although it was a friendly family club, it was also a well-oiled machine in terms of the way it was run.

It wasn't just a case of the odd executive box, there were rows of them and a restaurant, which was a big draw through the week as well as doubling up to host the Vice-President's Club on match days. The restaurant even received a mention in Egon Ronay's *Good Food Guide* at the time, so the club was making a name for itself as a forward-thinking outfit.

We really only saw Highfield Road on match days, since Coventry already had their own training centre at Ryton, a large swathe of ground on what I believe used to be a quarry on the edge of the city. It was another of Jimmy Hill's innovations, funded by the chairman, Derrick Robbins, in the 1960s. The complex covered tens of acres and was brilliant, self-contained and an ideal base for the team through the week. We had our pick of lush training pitches right through the year, a stark contrast to the Albion back in Glasgow, where the so-called all-weather pitch would flood at the first sign of rain.

Although Highfield Road was a neat and tidy little ground, the playing surface was pretty generous and certainly no smaller than Anfield or Highbury. There was a feeling that the supporters were close, but it wasn't an intimidating place in the mould of Ibrox or Parkhead. I'd come from an environment where the passion was unparalleled and walked into a set-up where the supporters, while right behind their team, were a bit more reserved and measured. It felt as though you had to work harder for your applause. The average crowd was around 20,000 and that took a bit of getting used to, but the way I was welcomed to the club and the city by supporters really made an impression on me. I still look forward to my trips back to Coventry, even if it is the Ricoh Arena rather than Highfield Road that us old-timers now have to get used to. The Ricoh's a wonderful football venue and that's the type of progress you can't argue against.

The only slight problem I had was with the Coventry kit. Obviously the home colours were sky blue, but the away strip was green and black, pretty much identical to Celtic's change strip at various points. Pictures of me in that Coventry jersey have raised a few eyebrows among Rangers fans over the years.

To say I was impressed by what I found at Coventry is an understatement. I don't know what I was expecting, but I got a pleasant surprise even before I'd been introduced to the squad. Once I got down to work, the good vibes continued, with a fine bunch of lads at the club. The quality was no less than I was used to at Rangers and if anything the strength in depth was greater at Coventry, with a lot of very talented players in the reserves who could easily have stepped up and done a job for the first-team.

Roy Barry was at the heart of the defence, a player I knew very well from our battles when he was with Dunfermline back in Scotland. He'd also played for Hearts, but it was with the Pars that he enjoyed his finest hour, captaining them when they won the Scottish Cup in 1968. He was skipper at Coventry, too, and although he was small for a centre-half, he was solid as a rock. Roy was a really tough defender, one you'd far rather have on your side than against you, so I was happy to land up his teammate at last. He was part of what turned into a colony of Scots, obviously led by Gordon Milne.

Gordon was a fantastic operator. His approach was very different from the Waddell–Wallace regime I'd left behind, preferring an arm round the shoulder to the strong-arm stuff I was more used to. I don't think it weakened his position any, because the majority responded well to it, and he had a quiet authority built on the fact we could see he knew the game inside out. Gordon was a tactician and cut his cloth to suit the situation.

Tommy Hutchison, who arrived for the same sort of fee as me, and at virtually the same time, was another of the Scottish contingent and far and away the most successful. Tommy was voted Coventry's greatest ever player by supporters not so long ago and he is idolised down there. With Hutch on the wing anything was possible, and when he received the ball you could sense the City fans holding their breath, waiting for something special to happen. Signing him from Blackpool was a stroke of genius by Gordon Milne. He knew what he was getting though, having played alongside him at Bloomfield Road, and it was an inspired decision to go back for him when he became a manager.

Hutch played on well into his 40s, seeing out his days in the Welsh league, and I'm staggered that he has never given management a crack. He heads up Bristol City's community coaching department and loves what he does, but if he ever fancied a change he'd be the ideal man to run a team; his knowledge of the game is first class.

Willie Carr from Glasgow and Brian Alderson from Dundee were also on the books, making it feel like a home from home, but we didn't take over completely, with the likes of Dennis Mortimer and our goalkeeper Bill Glazier important to the team.

What Gordon was trying to do was reinforce a squad that, in the main, had been home reared. So many of the team I joined at Coventry had never played football anywhere else, including the likes of Michael Coop and Bob Parker, and sometimes you need a shot of fresh blood to introduce new ideas and keep everyone on their toes.

I arrived a few months into the season, when Coventry were fourth from bottom of the league, but we went on a run and shot up to third at one stage before losing momentum towards the end of the season.

My debut was down in London against Crystal Palace. Up to that point, we had won only twice in 11 games but we beat Palace 1–0 and then picked up steam, being unbeaten in the next seven league matches and clocking up some important results.

We beat Arsenal 2–0 at their place, as well as taking full points against Everton and Manchester City.

Results like that backed up my initial assessment that I had landed on my feet in a squad capable of making an impact, but there was still a period of adjustment for me because it was a different ball-game in England.

With the best will in the world, Coventry were never going to go to places like Anfield or Highbury and dictate to Liverpool and Arsenal, so we worked on the basis that we would have to make ourselves difficult to beat in the first instance. It was a more compact style of play for me than previously, and there were fewer scoring chances than had been created for me in Scotland, but I enjoyed the challenge.

I'd gone from a league where I knew every defender inside out to a totally different environment. Virtually every opponent was new to me, but I soon found out all about them.

It was a blessing that the arrival of Tommy Hutchison and I

coincided with that nice run of form, because it eased the pressure on us.

I didn't enjoy the good fortune to score a hat-trick to match my Rangers debut, but I settled quickly enough to ensure that the fans were on my side. I felt I had to prove myself all over again, having been parachuted in with a big reputation but no track record in English football. I scored in the win against Manchester City in what was only my second game and that helped settle my nerves, especially since it was at Highfield Road.

It was a wonderful fixture to have as my first home game for Coventry, because it helped blow away the last lingering doubts about the path I'd taken and focus me totally on the new job in hand.

When you leave Rangers, the only way is down and technically I could have dug my heels in at Ibrox and refused to go. I didn't want to end up at odds with the club, so I followed their wishes. I'd been well and truly sent to Coventry.

I looked around the pitch that day against Manchester City and for the first time in the couple of weeks I had been down in England I began to think, 'I could get used to this.' There was a good crowd that day, more than 25,000 people, and on the opposite side of the pitch as we lined up were City legends like Rodney Marsh, Mickey Summerbee, Franny Lee and Colin Bell. If I'd still been with Rangers, I would have been away at Motherwell and it is fair to say that the company wouldn't have been quite so glamorous. We won the game 3–2, with little Brian Alderson scoring the winner after I'd put my name on the scoresheet. Marsh and Summerbee chipped in with a goal apiece for City.

The opposition that day were a far better team going forward than they were sitting back, but I soon found out that not every side was like that; the very next game was right into the lion's den, away to Leeds United.

I'd felt the pain of the Leeds machine when I was crocked by Billy Bremner years earlier as a Hibs player and he was still in the team when I went back in Coventry colours. He didn't get too close that time, but I had enough to contend with trying to stay one step ahead of Jack Charlton and Norman Hunter who wasn't known as 'Bites Yer Legs' for nothing. The thing with Norman and most of the other hardmen down in England was that they didn't chirp away at you in the same way as defenders would in Scotland. They didn't say a word, but you soon knew about it when they hit you. Charlton and Hunter were tough customers and I always found Phil Neal at Liverpool a really difficult man to get the better of. Every game presented you with another set of problems to try to solve, and I loved it.

The incredible thing at that time was the number of Scottish players operating south of the border. Not long after I arrived, we went down to play Arsenal, who were aiming for the title, and I caught up with my old Hibs mate Peter Marinello. We didn't do him any favours mind you, winning 2–0 at Highbury, and it was one of the results that cost them dear, given that they lost out to Liverpool in the championship by just three points. Peter was playing in a team with Frank McLintock and George Graham, and practically every side had a core of Scots.

I like to think we held our own and certainly that first season I spent down at Coventry worked well for our little tartan contingent. I played every game after signing and scored twelve goals, roughly one in every three games. Brian Alderson was ahead of me with 16 goals and Hutchison was a big hit straight away. Brian was stick-thin and all of 5ft 7in tall, but he could hit a ball like he had a sledgehammer in his boots. He reminded me of Andy Penman in that respect, because his power took you by surprise. We struck up a good partnership and scored a lot of goals between us in that first season.

Unfortunately, our results tailed off in the second half of the season and we endured a horrible run to the summer. We slid out of the top half of the table and ended up losing our last seven on the bounce, staying up on the back of our form earlier in the season and beating relegation by five points. It was Crystal Palace and West Brom who went down and there was a big feeling of relief all around the club.

I was used to a different pressure, the expectation of winning trophies and challenging for the league, but the fear of relegation is actually far more difficult to deal with. We all felt we had a better squad than the results in the last couple of months of the season suggested, and we went away for our holidays determined to put it right the following season.

15

Sir Alf's tartan two

My name has appeared in quite a few pub quizzes over the years, but there's one piece of trivia that I'm particularly proud of. Can you name the two Scottish players used by Sir Alf Ramsey in international football? I was one and the other was Peter Lorimer.

The occasion fell a few months into my time with Coventry, during a challenge match to celebrate the entry of Britain, the Republic of Ireland and Denmark to the European Union, or the Common Market as it was back then.

Sir Alf was, perhaps not surprisingly, chosen to lead the home team out at Wembley in January 1973 and he put together a pretty impressive squad of players to face a team picked from the six existing member countries of France, Italy, West Germany, Belgium, Holland and Luxembourg. Mind you, poor old Luxembourg didn't get a look in.

I've still got the letter informing me of the call-up and listing the rules and protocol we had to follow. Sir Alf was nothing if not organised and every corner was covered, even although it wasn't a competitive fixture. We each received a £100 appearance fee, which wasn't bad at all for a day's work, and before we reported for duty we were issued with a rule book. Everything was covered, from when we were allowed our last drink in the days leading up to the game to the strict policy on not speaking to the media beforehand. We actually had a similar set of guidelines at Coventry and it worked if you had the boundaries there in black and white, so you knew if you stepped over them you'd be hammered.

Peter and I were the only Scots who made the cut for the Common Market game and it was a real pleasure to play alongside some of the greats from home and abroad. Pat Jennings was in goal, with Peter Storey, Emlyn Hughes, Colin Bell, Bobby Moore, Bobby Charlton, Allan Hunter and Johnny Giles completing the British contingent. Henning Jensen, who played his football in Germany, also made the starting 11, with Alan Ball on the bench.

We travelled down individually to Lancaster Gate in London and were bussed out to the Homestead Court Hotel in Welwyn Garden City, where we had a two-night stay leading up to the game. We trained in Stevenage in the days before the match under Sir Alf, where he prepared us for the 4-3-3 formation he planned. It was new to me, and even in that one game I learnt from the man. By then, he was well past the honeymoon period that followed the 1966 World Cup win, but still commanded respect in any dressing room. Dispensing with wingers, especially when you are in charge of a country with such a proud tradition in that department thanks to the efforts of Sir Stanley Matthews and Sir Tom Finney, takes courage and conviction.

The match was billed as The Three versus The Six and there were some great names pulled together by the visitors. They included Dino Zoff, a certain Berti Vogts, my old adversary Franz Beckenbauer and his Germany teammate Gerd Muller, as well as Johan Neeskens flying the flag for the Netherlands and the French striker Georges Bereta. Johan Cruyff was also due to play, but pulled out through injury. He still flew into London with The Six though and was at Wembley, looking every inch the superstar in his smart leather jacket and exuding the type of confidence that sets the Dutch apart, for the post-match banquet.

Although it was a friendly fixture, the big names pulled in a healthy crowd and we needed a police escort to get us to the ground on time. I was able to repay Sir Alf's faith by scoring one of the goals in our 2–0 win, with Denmark's Henning Jensen adding the other. The abiding memory isn't of the goal, as welcome as it was, but of Alan Ball's shouts for the ball. He really is as high-pitched as he's made out to be! To run out at Wembley wearing what was near enough an England kit wasn't something I'd ever expected as a proud Scot, but there I was, resplendent in all white. Thankfully, the No. 13 I'd been handed turned out not to be unlucky for me.

With so much talk about a combined British team competing in the Olympics, it would be interesting to see how many Scots would make it. Peter and I certainly enjoyed the experience and it put a spring in my step going into the last few months of the season. When any player moves to a new league, they are desperate to establish themselves, and I was no different. When I received the call from Sir Alf, it gave me an idea that I had been accepted in England and that I was going about things the right way.

The summer of 1973 gave the Steins the opportunity to start calling England home. After nine difficult months apart, catching a few days together when we could, I was back together again with Linda and Nicola. We began house-hunting and Joe Mercer, typically of the man, came with us to smooth the way. You can imagine what the householders thought when they swung open the front door to find Joe, who was one of English football's best known personalities, staring back at them. Their faces were a picture, but Joe and his wife went out of their way to make our move south go smoothly.

We soon found our new home in Kenilworth, a lovely Warwickshire town just a 10-mile drive from Coventry. Willie Carr was in the next village and Tommy Hutchison and Roy Barry were nearby in Allesley, so it was a very social set-up. Kenilworth itself is a quiet suburb, best known for its castle, and perfect for a young family.

We bought a lovely house in the town thanks to the Coventry

stalwart Mick Coop, who tipped me off that a friend of his was selling up and it turned out to be just what Linda and I were looking for. There's a nice golf-course in Kenilworth, perched up on the hillside with views over the county for miles around, and a brand spanking new clubhouse had just been built when we moved down. I spent many happy hours out on the course there and was made to feel so welcome, just as the family was wherever we went in the area. Obviously, we wondered if we were doing the right thing to start with, but as soon as we were together in England we knew we had.

It was a totally different way of life and I have to admit that it appealed to me. I had become used to the fact that I couldn't go out in Glasgow, but in Coventry it was different. Tommy Hutchison had been put up in the same hotel as me when we both joined the club so we struck up a good friendship, killing the countless spare hours we had together. The pair of us used to drink in a bar called the Devonshire Arms, run by a brilliant Irishman called Bill Martin. It was a big, old inn near to the city centre and always busy, but we never had a minute's bother and enjoyed some great nights there. People would come up and say hello and there would be banter with opposition fans, but they never turned abusive in the way I'd had to put up with as an Old Firm player. Bill's retired from the pub now, but he still has an executive box at the club and I see him from time to time at the Ricoh Arena when I'm back for the reunions.

He was one of the good friends I made in England and the whole experience was an enjoyable one. Although we were a fair distance from home, the warmth of the welcome we received made sure it didn't feel that way. Willie Johnston wasn't a million miles away, either, playing with West Brom by that point, and although we met up a few times we were both so quickly accepted by everyone in our adopted cities that we didn't have to look back to the good old days for comfort.

The fact that I'd often see groups of Rangers supporters

coming along to the Coventry games to cheer me on helped, too. There were a lot of Rangers supporters clubs in the south and quite a few would stop off in the Midlands to take in our games when they didn't go the whole hog and motor up to Glasgow, so I'd put a few tickets aside for them.

Of course, it was football that had taken me to Coventry, not the surroundings or the way of life. Things were as different at work as they were at home and that really began to hit home at the start of my first full season with the club, the 1973/74 campaign.

I had been used to Jock Wallace and Murder Hill for pre-season, so I rolled up in the summer of 1973 fearing the worst. What Gordon Milne had in store for us was very different though, with the emphasis on short, sharp drills rather than the stamina tests I had been brought up on. At Rangers you wouldn't see a ball for days on end because of the total devotion to building fitness at the beginning of every pre-season, but at City there was a far more relaxed approach to that side of training. The benefit for me was that the core fitness I'd built up in the years previously never left me, so I was out in front of the pack when we did do the occasional piece of distance running.

The pre-season training programme was a reflection of Gordon's view on the game and part of it was also to do with the style of English football in general. I found it was a different proposition from Scotland and I spent far more time with my back to goal than I ever had before. Rather than running onto through balls I was far more involved in the build-up play, playing as a link man a lot of the time because there were fewer players going forward in support. Instead of looking for the quick attack, I had to learn to be more patient. At Rangers, I was used to the team having 80 per cent of the ball and creating the same proportion of chances in every game, whereas with Coventry it was far more nip and tuck in each match. That wasn't a bad thing and helped improve my all-round game.

Training was not the only big difference I had to adapt to, expectation was another. I'd come from a club where second-best was not good enough and had to settle into a side with far more modest ambitions. I don't think it necessarily shone through in the attitude of the players, but there was acceptance from outside that we would not win certain matches.

That said, we caused plenty of upsets along the way and showed the potential that there was within the squad. The first couple of games in the 1973/74 season pitched us up against Spurs and Liverpool and we won them both. The big problem, yet again, was finding any consistency. We went from beating Liverpool to drawing against the likes of Burnley, so any hopes of challenging at the top were dented by indifferent performances against sides we should have been beating.

I can't emphasise enough how much quality we had in that squad as well as in the youth team and reserves, reward for the time and money spent on bringing through young players. Just as they had in so many other areas, the club stole a march when it came to rearing its own players. There was a hostel for the kids who were brought in from far and wide, it was a football academy long before that particular phrase had been coined.

Bob Dennison was Gordon Milne's assistant and was a wise old owl. Bob was in his 60s when I arrived and although his job title suggested he was on first-team duty, his real passion was with the up-and-coming players. He played a big part in scouting and brought some excellent youngsters to Coventry. He has a tremendous thirst for knowledge and nine times out of ten you would find him with his head buried in a newspaper, with another dozen different papers sitting in a pile next to him. Bob never set the heather alight as a player, but he'd managed at Middlesbrough before joining Gordon at Highfield Road and he was well-regarded by the players.

Coventry found great success with bringing players through the ranks, many being sold at a big profit. Dennis Mortimer

went on to win the European Cup with Aston Villa, but the big
surprise to me is that more players, young and old, weren't
cherry-picked from Highfield Road over the years.

I was certain Willie Carr would end up at Manchester United
or one of the other big guns, but it didn't happen. Willie did go
on to give Wolves sterling service after leaving Coventry at
around the same time as I did. Tommy Hutchison would have
graced any team in the land, but stayed loyal to City for the best
part of a decade.

Even with players like that to call on, the attempts to break
into the top half of the league proved frustrating. I had my own
personal problems to contend with, too, as the 1973/74 season
was interrupted by a series of injuries.

I had never missed more than the odd game through injury
here or there in my life. The only real scare I had was when I was
knocked unconscious in a game against Kilmarnock down at
Rugby Park. When I woke up I could only feel my toes and the
tips of my fingers, nothing else. It was a horrible experience, but
the recovery was quick, unlike when I suffered the first of my
problems at Coventry.

I tore my hamstring badly and was forced to rest for weeks on
end. For someone who loved training and playing, it was
difficult to be on the sidelines for the first time and I didn't
need pushed when the manager asked me to try to get myself fit
for a big game against Arsenal. On the eve of the match, our
physio Norman Pilgrim put me through a fitness test but when I
ran full pelt, it went again, I swear I could hear it go ping. In
hindsight, I can see that it was the beginning of the end for me as
a player, even though I was still only 27 at that point. I don't
blame Norman or the club in the slightest. I was pushed to try to
get back sooner than I was ready, but only because I was so keen
to play. I wanted to make it back, they wanted me back, but it
wasn't to be.

It took another spell on the treatment table and kicking my

heels on the sidelines to recover, but when I eventually did return there was a nagging doubt in the back of my mind about whether I was fully over the injury. It was because I'd never had any sort of trouble before that I had concerns, but it wasn't helped by the fact I was also carrying an ankle injury.

I'd taken a whack in a game and although there was no serious damage, it gave me a lot of pain and discomfort from then on. I scored most of my goals with my right foot, albeit with a couple of memorable exceptions, and it was my right ankle that was bothering me. I needed it strapped up before every game and the knock I'd taken obviously compounded the wear and tear from 10 years in the game.

The ankle was a niggling injury, but it was the hamstring that gave me greater concern. Inside, I felt I'd lost a yard or two of pace, and given that acceleration was such a big part of my game, I knew it would catch up with me eventually. I'd always had explosive pace, with the first couple of yards where the race was usually won, and to feel that fading was a big worry and something I began to compensate for by adapting the way I played slightly.

I battled back with Coventry and we finished a rollercoaster ride of a league campaign in sixteenth place. It was as strange a season as I've ever experienced; we were just a couple of points clear of relegation, yet 10 points off third place. Manchester United went down in that 1973/74 season, which puts Coventry's achievement of maintaining top-flight football for so long into perspective.

Leeds United under Don Revie reigned supreme that year. It was Revie's last season with the club and they were like a machine, relentless from the first kick of the ball to the last. They only lost one game at Elland Road all season and didn't drop many points on the road either. We held them to a 0–0 draw at Highfield Road, but nobody was going to stop them, not even the great Liverpool team of the time. Liverpool finished runners-up, and Revie had his hands on the prize to sign off in style before taking on the England job. Leeds self-destructed after that, when Brian Clough and a succession of other managers came in, but at their peak they were a formidable side to play against.

English football was incredibly competitive at the time, and locally the rivalry was just as intense. West Brom, even with Willie Johnston on board, had been relegated the season I arrived in England and didn't come back up again while I was south of the border, but within the Midlands we still had derbies against Leicester, Wolves and Birmingham in the First Division, and they were all big games. Obviously it wasn't a patch on the Old Firm, but a derby is a derby wherever you are in the world and I loved playing in those fixtures. Molineux and St Andrews in particular were great grounds to play at, intimidating places to go to as an opposition team, but proper football grounds with really intense supporters. I was fortunate to play in England at a time when hooliganism wasn't an issue. The supporters directed their passion in the right way, so there was little trouble even when feelings were running high on the terraces.

Unfortunately, there were bigger problems to deal with in the Midlands. In the winter of 1974 the region ground to a halt when the news broke that 21 people had died in the Birmingham pub bombings. Nearly 200 people were injured and throughout the area there was a real sense of fear. The IRA threat had already been close to home in the run-up to the Birmingham attack, when a bomber had been killed trying to plant a device in Coventry's telephone exchange, but the scale of the tragedy really rammed home how real the situation was.

It was an uncomfortable time for everyone, but in a sense it brought the cities closer together and football helped with that process, too. Wolves held the bragging rights in the Midlands at the end of the 1973/74 season, but they only finished a few points above us and going into the next campaign there was another spending spree at Highfield Road.

The rise to the top league had been helped in no small way by the financial backing of Derrick Robins, who was the chairman and then, when he handed that role over to his son Peter, president at City. Derrick was big in cricket at the time, breaking apartheid to take English touring sides to South Africa in the early 1970s, but most importantly in terms of finances, he was big in the building industry. It was there that he had made his fortune and he ploughed large chunks of it into his football club over a lengthy period of time.

Robins bankrolled Jimmy Hill's plans on and off the pitch and continued to dig deep after Hill left. In the summer of 1974, another club record was broken when Larry Lloyd signed from Liverpool for £210,000, and as a player that was heartening. It sent out the message that the board was still desperate for success and as signings go, they couldn't have produced a bigger one than Larry, in every sense.

He was 6ft 2in and an absolute giant of a defender. It reached the stage where I would just stand aside at corners, because when he came up to join the attack you didn't want to be the man who got in his way. You'd end up picking your teeth off the floor. Larry was as uncompromising as they come, a real man's man. He had already won the Uefa Cup with Liverpool and was an England international when he arrived, so it was big news for Coventry. Larry went on to win the European Cup with Nottingham Forest, too, so you can't argue with his record.

He was brought in to join a defence led by our club captain, John Craven, who took over that job when Roy Barry left for Crystal Palace at the start of the previous season. John had come in from Palace himself but didn't stay long, leaving a couple of years after I did to join Plymouth.

When we started the season in the summer of 1974, he was the man with the armband, but it was passed to me during that season. John fell out of the team through injury and Gordon Milne called me into his office at the Ryton training ground to ask me how I felt about taking over as the skipper.

I didn't need asking twice, it was a great honour. I hadn't captained a side before and it was a privilege as well as a sign of the regard the manager held me in, the type of vote of confidence every player is happy to receive. I know a lot of people have argued that the captaincy of any club is a burden they can live without, it can be hard enough looking after yourself at times never mind a whole team, but I never found it a chore.

I was fortunate enough to play under some great skippers, from Joe Davis at Hibs and John Greig at Rangers to Roy Barry at Coventry, and I leant on those experiences. Really, all you can do is try to lead by example and I hope I did that.

There were certainly plenty of opportunities for team bonding in English football. We may not have had the European adventures that brought us together at Rangers, but there were plenty of long road trips to places like Ipswich, Norwich and Southampton. We would stay overnight for those fixtures and we had a good bunch of players at Coventry, so the time flew past. I've listened to players in Scotland complain about trips to the likes of Aberdeen, but until you've been on the road in England you don't know what travelling is – you could be in Southampton one week and Newcastle a few days later, so the miles were quickly clocked up.

Every trip also allowed me to tick off another ground on my list. There were some fantastic venues, with West Ham's Upton Park and the Dell in Southampton among my favourites in terms of atmosphere. Of course, Anfield and Old Trafford took some beating and were on a different scale completely, but every ground had its own appeal. To have played at those places and been fortunate enough to score a few goals into the bargain is something I'll always look back on.

As well as taking on the captaincy for my last season at Highfield Road, I also took on penalty-taking duties for a spell. I've never made a secret of the fact I wasn't 100 per cent comfortable from the spot, but the manager was keen for me to take them and I had a good success rate. I remember scoring one in a win against Arsenal and then another the following week in a draw against Liverpool, so maybe I should have stepped up more often in my Rangers days. I'd missed from the spot in a game down at Kilmarnock once and when Willie Waddell came marching into the dressing room, he told me I'd never take another one again. Those words were still at the back of my mind when I was down at Coventry, but I proved my point in the end.

As captain, penalty-taker and the main striker, it looked as if things were building up nicely for me at Coventry. I should have known by then that the path in football doesn't always take the direction you expect and there was another big twist just around the corner.

16

A glorious homecoming

How's your f***ing fitness? Jock Wallace was never one for standing on ceremony and with that question he welcomed me back to Rangers in the spring of 1975 after a totally unexpected turn of events. Just as I'd been taken aback by the speed of my departure from Ibrox less than three years earlier, I was caught completely on the hop when it was time to return to the club I will always class as home.

Funnily enough, my thought process was much the same when the contract was put on the table to bring me back – all I wanted to know was where to sign. A lot of water had passed under the bridge since I had first become a Rangers player, but nothing had taken away my passion. Once you wear that light-blue jersey, nothing can replace the buzz you get from it.

I loved my time in England with Coventry. We may not have won trophies or been playing in Europe, but I came away with some wonderful memories from that period of my life. In one sense, it was a real wrench to leave because the whole family had settled in Warwickshire; little Nicola had the most beautiful English accent and my son Martin had not long been born. On the other hand, I was presented with the opportunity to become part of a football institution again and in such a short career you can never afford to turn your back on chances like that.

I was out on the golf-course down in Warwickshire, totally oblivious to the negotiations going on behind the scenes, when I received a message that the morning papers in Scotland were full of headlines about Colin Stein and Rangers. There had been a call to the clubhouse and when I got in from my usual round, the members were all wondering what the story was. I had to tell them the truth. I really didn't have a clue.

Soon enough, I got word from City and sat down to talk to Gordon Milne. He told me straight that Rangers wanted me back and that Coventry had agreed a package to make the transfer happen. I later discovered that it was far more compli- cated than it appeared, but all of the fine detail was kept from me. The bottom line was that the clubs were happy for me to switch sides and the decision was on my shoulders.

On paper it could have been difficult. I had the choice of staying put with a club I had developed great affection for and who were paying me a salary beyond my wildest dreams, with a manager who had me as one of the first names on his team sheet and who had made me captain, while living in a part of the world where we had been welcomed with open arms. The alternative was to go back to play for a manager who had sold me just a couple of seasons earlier, to a city where I knew life was far from straightforward for a football player and to a team that already had a settled forward line.

It should have been a no-brainer, the sensible option would have been to refuse point-blank and play on with Coventry. But I was never one to do things the easy way, and the lure of playing for Rangers again was impossible to resist. I told Gordon I was keen to go and before I knew it, the pair of us were in a car along with Eddie Plumley, the club secretary, heading up the road to Glasgow. I don't know if I expected a red carpet at Ibrox, but what I received was the Wallace welcome.

His opening gambit about my fitness was maybe a bit brash, but in actual fact it was spot on. He had good cause to be worried about my physical condition, because I hadn't played for a few weeks when they made their move, recovering from another of the little niggles that had crept into my game.

The flip side was that I had already crammed in twenty-four league games and a couple of cup ties that season and with seven goals was just one off Brian Alderson at the top of the Coventry scoring table, so my form was strong enough. The standard in English football was high and if you can score goals down there then you'll be able to do the same in Scotland.

Mind you, Jock knew as well as anyone what I was capable of when I was on song and the only doubt in his mind was whether or not I could still play at the same tempo and with the same power. I'd only been away for around 30 months, but that's a long time in football. He was well aware of the ankle and hamstring injuries I'd suffered and would also have known the impact that being out of his strict training regime would have on any player.

For the first time in my life, I was put through a fitness test before putting pen to paper. It was like going back to my schooldays, when I had trials with junior sides, as I pulled on my trainers to go out on the track with Tom Craig, the physio. Tommy put me through my paces for a good while, running me every way he could. Inside I felt I had lost a bit of speed and I'm sure he must have been thinking the same thing as he watched me go through the routine. But Tom didn't say anything to Jock, he passed me fit to sign. In truth, it was the right thing because there was nothing physically wrong, it was simply a case of Old Father Time beginning to get the better of me.

I suppose neither Tom nor Jock was expecting the old Colin Stein and they were content enough with what they saw to push the deal through. True to form, Jock ran me into the ground in training to get me back into the swing of things and prepare me for my second debut.

While all that was going on, what I wasn't aware of was the turmoil I was leaving behind at Coventry. I later discovered that

the president, Derrick Robins, who had been the money man
behind the rise up the leagues, had told his board he was retiring
and moving to South Africa. He took his chequebook with him
and as a result the directors were already battening down the
hatches. They couldn't keep up the repayments on the instal-
ment plan they had agreed when they signed me from Rangers,
so had no choice but to sell me back. Rangers paid them
£80,000, I presume to cover the money they had received
from Coventry for my original transfer, and the account was
settled. There was no pressure put on me to agree to go back,
but I've often wondered what would have happened if I hadn't
been keen. I would imagine it would all have got a bit messy
between the clubs, but fortunately it never came to that. It was
when Robins left that Jimmy Hill returned to Highfield Road,
initially as managing director, so as one chapter closed another
opened for the Sky Blues.

At the start of my final season with the club, Joe Mercer had
taken a step back from the football side at Coventry, moving
onto the board and serving as a director into the early 1980s.
Gordon Milne stayed just as long and he had some good times
with Coventry. The year I left, they finished thirteenth in the
First Division, continuing the progress we had made over the
previous few seasons, and over time the club became established
as a fixture in the First Division. What Gordon brought more
than anything was stability, and you can't put a price on that. He
was in the top job for seven years and when you consider that in
the seven years after he left in 1981 another five managers tried
to fill his shoes, you get an idea of how important he was to the
club. He brought in something like £4 million in transfer fees
and had a knack of unearthing gems that he could polish and sell
on. It kept the club afloat when times were hard, but fans don't
always appreciate that side of the business.

It was no surprise at all that Gordon went on to bigger and
better things, using Leicester City as a springboard to overseas

football. The success he had, particularly with Besiktas in Turkey where he won a clutch of trophies, was no more than he deserved. Gordon had a great talent for making football easy. His methods were simple but there was a purpose to everything he did and the fact he kept what was a provincial club in among the big boys of the First Division for so long is a ringing endorsement of his ability as a coach. From the day I left Coventry, I have always followed their fortunes. I must have been the only man in West Lothian celebrating when they won the FA Cup in 1987, but I'll always have a soft spot for them.

I still get a good reception when I go down for the Legends days that the club hosts at the Ricoh Arena and I enjoy those trips immensely. The new stadium is absolutely tremendous and true to Jimmy Hill's vision for Highfield Road decades ago, it is far more than just a football ground, in use every day of the week. It is a crying shame that the club doesn't have Premier League football to go with the facilities, because they certainly wouldn't be out of place. It pains me to see them struggling in the bottom half of the Championship, but there seems to be optimism now that they can move in the right direction and aim to get back to the top division sooner rather than later.

My visits south always bring the memories flooding back and although Coventry has changed a lot since the 1970s, there are enough reminders around the city to make it feel like the home it was to me all those years ago. I left so suddenly that I didn't have too much time to take it all in. When I played my last batch of games early in 1975, I had no inkling that I would be leaving that spring. My last goal in English football was down at White Hart Lane when we drew 1–1 against Tottenham at New Year, and I only played a handful of games after that. The last one was a good way to sign off, with Highfield Road packed for an FA Cup match against Arsenal. We held them to a 1–1 draw and received a wonderful reception going off the pitch that day. I didn't realise then that it would be the last time I'd play at Highfield Road.

The next time I pulled my boots on I was in familiar surroundings back at Ibrox. After getting the paperwork completed, I found I settled quickly back into life at Rangers, not least because of the familiar faces who were around me. John Greig was still ruling the dressing room, with Sandy Jardine as his trusted lieutenant. Colin Jackson and Derek Johnstone were both going strong and in midfield Tommy McLean and Alex MacDonald were still running rings round the opposition. Alex Miller, who was just starting out when I left for Coventry, had begun to establish himself by the time I returned and they all made it easy for me to slot back in.

They hadn't done too shabbily in the time that I had been away. In the season I left, Rangers won the Scottish Cup and when I signed, I joined a team sitting proudly at the top of the league. They had barely been out of first position all season, although there was a slight wobble at the turn of the year when Celtic took over, but there was a real air of expectancy throughout Rangers circles as the end of the season drew near.

I could sense a totally different atmosphere in Glasgow from when I left. Although we had won in Europe just before I moved to Coventry, there was a real tension among the supporters because of the dominance Celtic had enjoyed in the league. In 1975 that tension had been replaced with excitement, because there was a real feeling that this was the year that the championship would be reclaimed after so many disappointments and near misses.

Things had changed within the club, too. Jock, who was still finding his feet as his own man in 1972 following Willie Waddell's move upstairs, had begun to stamp his authority and personality on the team and on the club. He was in charge now and he would live or die by his results.

The squad had evolved, not least in the striking department.

When Willie Johnston and I moved aside, the door swung open for Derek Parlane to establish himself as the main man and he didn't disappoint. He became an instant hero and was the leading scorer for three seasons on the trot. Where they had struggled was in finding a regular partner for Derek. He had played up alongside Derek Johnstone on occasion, but DJ had too big a part to play further back at that point to be committed full-time to playing up front.

The defence had been reshaped pretty dramatically from Barcelona. I came back into a side with Stewart Kennedy in possession of the goalkeeper's jersey. Willie Mathieson had gone, too, replaced by either John Greig or Alex Miller, depending on who was available, and Dave Smith was also no longer there. In his place was a very different type of player in Tom Forsyth, who was the total opposite to Dave in the way he played the game.

Quintin Young had taken over the No. 11 shirt vacated by Willie Johnston a couple of years previously and although nobody could ever replace Bud, he gave it a damn good shot. Cutty Young and I got on like a house on fire, rooming together, albeit briefly, but it turned out that the clock was ticking on his Rangers career.

Cutty was a bit of a tearaway in his heyday and it all came to a head when Graham Fyfe's wife called the club to say that he had gone AWOL. It turned out that he was down in Ayr with Cutty and the pair of them had painted the town red. As the elder of the two, Jock Wallace threw the book at Quintin and gave him his marching orders. Graham, who they obviously felt had been led astray by his more experienced sidekick, got off with a bit of a verbal kicking and was allowed to stay on the books.

The other new face, on the opposite side of the midfield, was Bobby McKean. The first I really saw of Bobby was when I came back to Rangers, because he was still a young boy. In training, I could see why Jock had been so keen to bring him in from St Mirren, he had everything a midfielder needed. Bobby was still in his 20s when he died in an accident at home just three years after we won the league back from Celtic, it was such a terrible waste of talent.

The average age of the team had been brought down and while it would be impossible to replace the likes of Smith, Johnston and Alfie Conn like for like, there was method in the way Jock had set about adding some more steel through the core of the side.

He parachuted me back into the side to play St Johnstone at Ibrox on a March afternoon. My arrival had caused a bit of a stir and I'll never forget the turnout that day. There were more than 42,000 at Ibrox to watch us play a middle-of-the-road Saints side and it was the biggest home crowd up to that point in the season, with the obvious exception of the Old Firm derby. All the old chants were ringing out and it brought home to me just what I'd been missing. To have Ibrox singing your name, fighting your corner, is a brilliant sensation. I was conscious before I left that I'd developed a cult following, but to still have the same level of support when I'd been away for more than two years was more than I could have hoped for.

We went into that game top of the league but with Celtic still hot on our heels. There were eight of the thirty-four league games to go and when you get to that stage of the season, every match becomes a difficult one. There was great play in the media about the fact that St Johnstone were aiming to make it 10 games in a row unbeaten in the First Division, but so were we. Celtic weren't playing until midweek, so Jock was determined to put two points on the board and heap the pressure on them. It was one of the youngsters, Ian McDougall, who made way for me in the team. I think the boss felt that he needed some steady nerves to see the job through. It was if I'd never been away when I ran out at Ibrox and I started throwing myself into the thick of things from the start. The pace of the game was quicker than I'd been used to in England and I had to get the feel for playing on the heels of the defenders again rather than dropping deep to hold the ball up. I'd loved every minute in England, but it was amazing how quickly I fell back into the old routine of getting forward at every opportunity. It didn't take long for the banter to start flying again either, with my old Hibs teammate Jimmy O'Rourke making sure I never got a second's peace. Jimmy was a real character and loved to give you a bit of stick on the park, good-natured stuff but enough to test your nerve. The key was to give as good as you got from him.

It wasn't an easy reintroduction to the Scottish game, but we got the result we had been sent out for, with Quintin Young scoring the only goal of the game. It stretched our lead over Celtic and when they lost up at Aberdeen in their Wednesday night game, it really began to slip away from them.

The next weekend we were on the road, away to Dundee. It was another potential banana skin because Dundee were no mugs, but we ground out a 2–1 win. It wasn't long after the full-time whistle that news began to filter through that Celtic had suffered another setback. I don't think a Dundee United win has ever been so well received at Dens Park, but we certainly had reason to celebrate United's 1–0 win at Parkhead. Andy Gray scored the only goal of the game and it looked as though the pressure was really beginning to take its toll on Celtic. The results that day meant that we moved a further two points ahead and the title was becoming a very real prospect. Confidence was sky high.

The next big step towards the prize was when we brushed Motherwell aside with a 3–0 win at Ibrox the following week. At the same time, Celtic lost 1–0 at Airdrie and all of a sudden it wasn't them we had to get the better of – Hibs jumped into the reckoning. My old side had been quietly putting together a decent run of results and that weekend they leapfrogged Celtic into second place. It was a dream for the papers because all of a sudden they had a huge match to look forward to: Hibs v Rangers at Easter Road, the title decider.

It was 29 March 1975 when we went through to Edinburgh for that match. There were five games to play and we were on 50 points, 9 ahead of Hibs and 10 clear of Celtic. The equation was simple. Hibs had to beat us to keep the league alive. A point would be enough for us to win the First Division.

Hibs had won their last three games and scored nine in the process, so Jock Wallace had us primed for a real battle. Jock was always wholehearted and hard, but in the build-up to that game there were small signs of just how much it meant to him. He was excited, probably nervous, and desperate to get it right.

John Greig, who had missed the previous match against Motherwell, was still out injured, so Alex Miller kept his place in the side and Sandy Jardine continued to deputise as captain. Hibs had my old mate Roy Barry at the heart of their defence, so I was relishing the opportunity to go head-to-head with him, knowing fine well he'd stick to me like glue all afternoon. Ally MacLeod and Pat Stanton were also still going strong and all of those experienced players must have realised that it was now or never for them.

The home team got off to the best possible start when Ally McLeod scored down at the bottom of the Easter Road slope. We thought we were back in the game when we won a penalty, but Sandy Jardine missed from the spot and it was back to square one.

Then it happened. Bobby McKean received the ball on the right and swung in a peach of a cross; it hung perfectly in front of me and I rose well to meet it flush with my head. For a second, everything felt as if it was standing still. Then the ball flew past Jim McArthur in the Hibs goal and the ground, which was absolutely packed with almost 40,000 people, erupted. There were Rangers supporters in every corner of the stadium, far outnumbering the home fans, and the celebrations spilled onto the pitch. They had waited 11 years to be crowned league champions and the relief when the ball hit the back of the net was as strong for them as it was for the players on the park.

With the clock running down, Jock Wallace gave John Greig the nod to get warmed up and the skipper was brought on from the bench to savour the occasion. Greigy was the only player left from the 1964 title-winning side and it was a nice touch by Jock to bring him on, even though he was injured. It was probably the one and only time I saw Jock's softer side, but at least it proved he had one.

When the full-time whistle went, it was absolute bedlam. Celtic had had the monopoly for so many years but our fans were ready to make up for lost time and the parties ran and ran for weeks afterwards. Everywhere you went, on every street and in every shop, people would throw their arms around you or shake your hand. There were a few refreshments taken by the players on the night of the Hibs game, but we couldn't go over the top. There were still four games to play and Jock wasn't going to let us off the leash until we had taken care of those. He wanted to stretch out the lead as much as possible before the end of the season, he wanted to lay down a marker. It wasn't just about that one season for him, he wanted to dominate for years to come and would knock his pan in to make it happen.

After Easter Road, we drew at Dundee United and I scored in wins against Aberdeen and Arbroath in the weeks after the Hibs game to set us up for the big one, the trophy presentation. It was a massive day for everyone connected with Rangers, but unfortunately Airdrie hadn't read the script and beat us 1–0.

Ibrox was jumping, full to capacity, and the result didn't matter one bit to the fans. The game was a side issue for them, they'd come to see the trophy being lifted. I can still remember standing in the middle of the park waiting for the presentation and all of us being gutted that we'd just lost the game. It's fair to say we were well-trained and losing any game, even the technically meaningless ones, hurt.

The final table read Rangers 56 points, Hibs 49. Celtic and Dundee United were tied on 45 points and the guard had changed. The blues were back on top, and it didn't half feel good.

17

My big regret

I am fortunate to have lived a life of very few regrets. I worked hard, played hard and walked away from football on my own terms. The one thing I do have to put right is the fact that I never made it to Jock Wallace's funeral, something I sincerely regret. One day soon I'll seek out Jock's grave and pay my respects to the man who caused me a whole lot of pain and anguish along the way, but who I always classed as a friend, not just my boss.

At times we fought like cat and dog, but through it all I never lost the respect I had for the man, and I think it was mutual. He called a spade a spade and while the truth sometimes hurt, especially when it was delivered in one of his brutal bursts, he was the way he was because he wanted the best for the club. The end results are difficult to argue with.

Like everyone else, I would curse him when he was pushing us to the limit, but he knew I could do the hard miles and he always had a place in his heart for those who could last the pace. His military background was never far from the surface and in football he wanted people in the trenches with him who were fit for battle. I like to think I never let him down in that sense, because I gave 100 per cent.

Jock served with the King's Own Scottish Borderers and if you were lucky enough to spend a bit of time with him, he would give little glimpses of his past through the odd tale here and there. He saw service in Malaysia and Northern Ireland. He was a man who had seen how tough life could be and how fortunate those of us who earned a living in football really were.

He didn't appreciate anyone who took that lifestyle for granted or who lost sight of what it meant to be a Rangers player.

When Willie Waddell took him to Rangers as his assistant in 1970, it was to complete his apprenticeship and Waddell was as good a teacher in the ways of Ibrox as anyone could have. He himself had learnt from the best in Bill Struth, and the traditions were passed down the line to Wallace, who upheld them with a passion. He took a gamble when he moved from his role as assistant at Hearts, where most people assumed he would succeed John Harvey as manager, to take on the same position with Rangers. But Jock was nothing if not confident, he obviously thought, why settle for the Hearts job when I can have the Gers one? Not for the first or last time, he turned out to be right. He was an outsider taken in by Willie Waddell to replace Harold Davis, an Ibrox hero. It was a tough assignment, but Jock took it in his stride, which was even more impressive since the Ibrox fans should have hated him. The fact that Jock played in goal for Berwick Rangers when they put Rangers out of the Scottish Cup in 1967 should have counted against him, but his passion overcame that potential sticking point and the fans could see how much the club meant to him. He was proud of that Berwick performance mind you, it probably ranked as the highlight of his playing career.

As a Midlothian boy, he grew up not a million miles from my home patch and we were similar characters in many ways. Both tough, both stubborn and both prepared to fight our corner. Not surprisingly, it led to more than one run-in between us, but the biggest was in the aftermath of the championship success in 1975.

When we moved to within an ace of the title, I chapped on Jock's office door and asked him if I would be one of the players to get a medal. He told me without even a second's hesitation that I wouldn't, that I hadn't been back long enough to deserve one.

I knew that was the case when we ran out at Easter Road, I knew that was the case when I was celebrating the goal that sealed the title. It was at the back of my mind then because the adrenalin of the occasion was pumping, but it really hit home when the rest of the squad were collecting their medals at Ibrox on the final day of the season. Sure enough, there was no box for me.

I argued with Jock beforehand about it and I argued about it after. But, as I knew in my heart of hearts, it was a fight I was never going to win. Jock didn't do compromise and he certainly never backed down. To this day, the decision not to award me a medal rankles. People still come up to me and say, 'You're the man who stopped 10-in-a-row.' It is just a pity I don't have a proper memento from that period.

I'm the first to acknowledge that most of the hard work had already been done by the time I came back to Ibrox, but we still had to get over the finish line and I played my part in that. I started every game after my transfer from Coventry, scoring three goals in eight games, nearly a quarter of the 34-game season. I couldn't have done any more than I did.

Stewart Kennedy and Sandy Jardine were ever present, but there were plenty of others who chipped in with appearances throughout the course of the season and I don't know how many of them were left without a medal. Only a dozen players made it into double figures for starting matches and I'd imagine there would have been more medals than that made available. In fact, Jock only used 19 players through the whole of that season.

Apparently, it was up to the club to decide which players got medals and ultimately it was at Jock's discretion. As far as he was concerned, I just hadn't done enough.

It became very heated between us but eventually, at the end of the season, I had to concede defeat. I decided to change tactic and went to Jock with what I felt was a decent solution. I offered to have my own medal struck and pay for it out of my own pocket. It seemed reasonable to me but not to him – he dismissed the suggestion out of hand and kicked me out of his office with my tail between my legs. He wasn't the most subtle of men and once he got going he turned the air blue, leaving you in no doubt what he was thinking.

I know exactly what a league winner's medal looks and feels like, because they're exactly the same as the Reserve League medal I won in the years that followed. Still, it would have been nice to receive the real deal. I'm half tempted to get the reserve one re-engraved to turn it into a First Division one. I watched recently when Jimmy Armfield, and the rest of England's reserves from the 1966 World Cup final collected their belated medals at Downing Street, so maybe there's hope for me yet!

It is something that hurt at the time and it still does. I've got cup-winner's medals, I've got my European badge and it's disappointing not to have a title medal to add to the collection. I even got a Scottish Cup runners-up medal in 1969 when I was suspended for the final, so I feel I would have been justified in getting one for the league in 1975.

For a few months I felt pretty cold towards Jock, but over time I mellowed a bit and it was business as usual between us. He was the man who sold me, denied me a medal, dropped me and eventually released me, yet I couldn't dislike him.

Long after we had both left the club, we joined forces again when I took part in a few events during his testimonial year, something Rangers Football Club had nothing to do with.

Jock, despite his service and the trophies he delivered, never had a benefit match awarded by the club. Instead, he had a testimonial organised independently and that just didn't sit right. I accompanied him at functions in Bo'ness and Tranent and saw supporters' club members dip into their pockets to donate. For such a proud man, it looked like an uncomfortable position to be in and I felt it was degrading for him.

That paled into insignificance when you compare it to the

way he was treated in the late 1980s, when he was thrown out of a lounge at Ibrox by club security. Apparently, he didn't have the right ticket, but after what that man did for the club he should have had a key to the door. I wasn't alone in feeling sickened by the way he was treated in later years, and it left a sour taste in the mouth of all of his former players. Yet Jock acted with dignity and never complained.

By the time the supporters arranged the testimonial year for him in 1994, the big man's health was beginning to fade and I just felt that Rangers should have done more. To be manager of Rangers is a special position and the club has a duty to look after its own. In Jock's case it didn't happen; even at his peak he was pretty poorly rewarded and that was the only reason he left for Leicester in 1978 on the back of his second treble.

The success he had at Leicester, winning the Second Division championship, and the respect he won in Spain when he managed Seville, suggests that his methods did not only work at Ibrox. I have to be honest and say I was surprised when Jock moved to Spanish football, because he came across as a home-body. But he was also a very astute coach and he won over the Seville players and supporters with his approach to the game. He liked steel first and foremost, with a bit of silk where appropriate. In the end, the language was a big barrier for him in Spain but at the same time I'd say some of his more colourful vocabulary would have been universal. He was a unique man and a talented manager.

It didn't shock me when he went back to Rangers for a second bite of the cherry in 1983 following John Greig's resignation as manager. As I know myself, it is very easy to let your heart rule your head when that chance rears up in front of you.

I also know that there's some sense in the old saying that you should never go back and I can't think of anyone who has really made a go of it at Rangers a second time, at least not in the long-term. I tried it, Derek Johnstone tried it and others have before and since. The lure of Rangers is just too strong, everyone thinks they are going to be the one that rewrites the rule book. Jock wasn't that man, unfortunately.

It must have hurt him when he was sacked in 1986 and it was a great shame that it came to that. He was operating under very difficult circumstances and anyone would have struggled. It didn't cloud what he had achieved previously, though. He was a treble-winning manager as well as a big part of the European success in 1972, and his track record stands up to the closest scrutiny.

When Jock stepped down from frontline duties in football in 1990, he had already been diagnosed with Parkinson's disease and although he tried to fight it, quite quickly he began to toil. In the end, it was a heart attack that cost him his life in 1996. The testimonial events were just a couple of years before he died and at least the Rangers supporters had the chance to express their appreciation. Nobody knew then how soon he would pass away. The funeral was, not surprisingly, a big affair, but I just didn't feel in the right frame of mind to go. Even although we knew he was ill, it still came as a big shock.

Four years earlier, I had been at Willie Waddell's funeral and it was a sad day. We all felt that the Barcelona team was invincible, but when Waddell passed away that feeling began to crumble. Losing Jock made that even more real, especially as he'd been such a strong character and was only 60 when he died. He was Rangers through and through and deserves to be remembered for what he was, a true blue.

18

The beginning of the end

When you have just played your part in a league-winning campaign, you should go away for your summer holidays feeling confident, relaxed and ready to take on the world. In fact I went away for the summer break in 1975 with doubts creeping into my mind about what the future held for me.

My fitness had been a worry for Rangers before they brought me back, but I'd blown away the concerns about my ability to stay injury-free. I was over the problems I'd endured at Coventry, but in my own mind I knew I was not as strong or as fast as I had been at my peak.

Bearing in mind that I was still only 28, it was difficult to come to terms with, but a player is the only person who can really judge their physical condition and I was honest enough to know that I was on the way down.

Jock Wallace was not a man for deep and meaningful one-to-one conversations, so there was no single moment when it became clear that I was not in his long-term plans. In fact, at the start of the 1975/76 season it appeared that I was very much in his thoughts. I sailed through pre-season training without a hitch and although I knew I was a yard or two slower when it came to pace, it would not have been too obvious to the coaching staff.

We went away to New Zealand and Australia on a pre-season tour and I played in just about every game. I scored a couple of goals and despite the concerns I had about my pace, I gained confidence and sharpness with every match I played.

The summer training camps became a tradition at the club and we were fortunate to visit some wonderful countries, including trips to Scandinavia and North America. A good tour could set you up for the season and the Barcelona year was a case in point. The summer before we won in Europe was spent in Sweden and it was out there that the team and formation we used to such great effect took shape. It was also where Derek Johnstone first shone as a defender, and in time that proved so vital.

The squad had been taken out to Sweden again before the league-winning season of 1974/75. Although that was before I returned from Coventry, I was back in time for the Australian trip in the summer of 1975 and it was a fantastic experience.

To say it was a tour of New Zealand and Australia isn't entirely accurate – we actually went via Canada. We stopped off in Vancouver to play British Columbia before flying on to the southern hemisphere for the tour proper, so it was a busy summer for us.

The first stop was New Zealand, for games in Auckland and Christchurch, before we moved on to Australia for matches in Sydney, Brisbane, Melbourne, Adelaide and Perth. It was a wonderful chance to see most of the country and we had some tough encounters down there, not least with the Australian national side when we played them in a double-header. That little contest ended in a draw, with one win each. The Socceroos had Jim Rooney, a Dundonian who had played junior football and with Montrose in the 1960s, in their side to add a bit of spice to it. Jim became a star in Australia after emigrating and he was their main man.

We played seven games in the space of 20 days in Australia and New Zealand and far from proving difficult, it was exactly what I needed. The older you get, the more you need games to keep you ticking over. I don't go with the theory that you can pull and push players in and out of the team to keep them fresh.

In those days, the season still started with the League Cup pool games, easing into the start of the league matches. Scottish football had been restructured after our championship win, with the Premier Division introduced and the number of teams in the top division cut from eighteen to ten. It meant playing each team four times, but in theory it should have led to a more competitive league, with the fringe teams cut of the equation and dropping down a level. Eventually, playing the same side four times a season became monotonous, but in the early days the novelty of the new structure was still fresh enough to keep it interesting.

It did mean we lost some familiar names from the top-flight, mind you. It was a killer for the sides who missed out that year, with Airdrie, Kilmarnock, Partick Thistle, Dumbarton, Dunfermline, Clyde, Morton and Arbroath all taking a tumble down to the new First Division. With the exception of Dumbarton and Arbroath, the majority of those clubs had a fan-base to support football at the highest level and it was a crushing blow for them to lose regular games against the Old Firm. Just a couple of matches against the big two would more or less cover their wage bill for the season and when that money dried up, it led to a lot of hard decisions at the fringe clubs.

Before we got stuck into the Premier Division fixtures against those who had survived the cull, we had six League Cup games to contend with. We were drawn in a group with Airdrie, Clyde and Motherwell. The big question was how Jock would accommodate the players he had. I was fully fit and raring to go, Derek Johnstone was champing at the bit and Derek Parlane had established himself as the club's leading scorer over the seasons. There were young players also knocking on the door and only a couple of forward positions to accommodate us all.

When the season kicked off, we found Jock was prepared to be bold. He fielded Derek Johnstone, Derek Parlane and myself in the same forward line. It worked too – we hammered Airdrie that day, banging six past them. I was one of the scorers and when you start the season in the team and on the score sheet, it gives you a lift at the perfect time.

The team as a whole was growing in stature and you could sense it was the start of something special, something that turned out to be a treble-winning season. We fired through the League Cup ties undefeated to qualify for the quarter-finals, but the manner in which we did it was just as important as the results. There were thumping wins, the 6–1 against Airdrie and a 6–0 against Clyde, and battling performances as well. It was a side capable of doing the dirty stuff as well as it could do the fast-attacking football when the time was right.

The championship flag was unfurled at an Old Firm game, to kick off the brave new era of the Premier Division. Ibrox was packed to bursting for the celebration, to see the flag over the ground for the first time since 1964. Derek Parlane picked up a knock before that game, so it was myself and Derek Johnstone leading the line that afternoon. DJ scored, as did Quintin Young, as we got off to a flyer with a 2–1 win.

What I didn't realise was that it would be the last game I would start for a while. When Derek Parlane returned the following week I was sacrificed, dropping down to the bench for the first time in my life. At Armadale, at Hibs, at Rangers the first time and at Coventry, I played in every game that I was available for. Now I had to learn to live with the fact that I wasn't going to be an automatic choice for Jock, and it was difficult to deal with.

I hated coming on as a substitute. You either got the shout to play when the team was chasing a lost cause or got a few minutes at the end of an easy win. For someone who thrived on being in the thick of things and changing games, it felt like the thin end of the wedge. I suppose I should have been grateful to be involved, but I couldn't see it like that. Still, I didn't sulk or make a big deal of it. I kept working away, training as hard as ever, and genuinely felt I could force my way back in.

It worked for me, although not in the way I expected. Jock came to me a couple of months into the season and told me he wanted me to drop back into midfield. Obviously my own theory about my pace fading was beginning to bear true in training and by playing me a bit deeper, the manager felt he could get round that problem.

With the fresher legs of Parlane and Johnstone up front, he wanted me to sit behind them and take advantage of the space they opened up with their clever running. The pair of them were a real handful for defenders and struck up a good partnership, so breaking them up was always going to be difficult once it had become clear that DJ's long-term future would be up front.

I'd always tried to bring more to the table than simply scoring goals, I liked to get involved as much as I could, so it wasn't alien to me to take on the extra responsibility. At Coventry under Gordon Milne, I'd had to work even harder at my all-round game because there were fewer chances and we had less of the ball. I was confident in my own ability to play in midfield, but never convinced it was where I could do the most damage or make the biggest contribution. Obviously, it was impossible to argue with the effectiveness of Parlane and Johnstone when they were on top form, so I did the best I could in the circumstances.

Moving to midfield was a path back into the team and for a month we gave it a good go. I played a couple of league games, including an Old Firm draw at Parkhead as we held our lead at the top, a couple of European ties and the League Cup final against Celtic as well.

I appreciated that final in October 1975 more than any other because by then I knew I had to savour every chance of playing in the big games. When you are young, you think you will play in finals every season, but with experience you realise it isn't the case. The fact that I'd spent a couple of seasons with a less fashionable club reinforced that. At Rangers, you are spoiled because success is all around you, but when you've seen the other side of the game, where survival is success, it is an eye-opener.

As usual there was a real sense of occasion surrounding the final. We were taken away to the Marine and Curlinghall Hotel in Largs to prepare and to keep us all under lock and key in the build-up to the game. Not that anyone could have got away with anything if we hadn't been spirited away to the seaside, because we were well watched throughout the season. The Ibrox doorman, Bobby Moffat, one of life's great characters, knew everything that was going on in Glasgow and particularly if it involved anyone on the Rangers payroll. He was the eyes and ears of a succession of managers and made sure we were looked out for while at the same time making sure that if anyone stepped out of line, the boss would find out. We knew it and, in the main, nobody would dare put a foot wrong. A few tried and, as Willie Henderson, Jim Baxter and Quintin Young discovered, they were soon on their bike.

Taking us away wasn't so much about keeping us in check, but more about bringing us together and away from distractions. The Marine and Curlinghall no longer exists, being demolished years ago, but in its heyday it was a wonderful place, the height of luxury and typical of the style we were accustomed to as Rangers players. Again, the Struth influence continued right through the decades, with his insistence on nothing but the best for the club's players not being lost on his successors. We used the hotel in Largs as our regular getaway for big games and it had everything we needed, from a putting green and snooker room to an in-house cinema. When you have a big game to look forward to, I always found boredom was the biggest enemy but we were kept busy down in Largs, with everything planned to the letter.

The build-up to the cup final was relaxed but businesslike. We felt we finally had the measure of Celtic so there was no trepidation amongst us. We felt we had the upper hand and would have played them every week if we could have.

Celtic were going through a transitional phase after the disappointment of their 10-in-a-row hopes being shattered. The likes of Danny McGrain, Kenny Dalglish and Bobby

Lennox were still going strong, but there was fresh blood introduced, including Peter Latchford in goal and Johannes Edvaldsson. Jock Stein had been seriously injured at the start of the season, so Sean Fallon took over the reigns while he recovered. It was a difficult time all round for them, but we paid little attention to what was happening at Celtic Park, it was what we did that counted.

It turned out to be the Alex MacDonald final, with Doddie scoring a cracking diving header from a Quintin Young cross midway through the second half to win the cup for us. It was a peach of a goal and no more than Alex deserved, a real crowning glory for him in a wonderful career. It was the first leg of the treble and got us off and running for the season. When you've got one trophy in the bag, it always gives you an edge and piles the pressure on the other team.

In the final, I was playing through the middle behind the two Dereks, although Jock also used me on the right side of midfield during that experimental period. It wasn't something I particularly enjoyed. Although I had played as a defender before I turned professional, I'd grown used to working as an out-and-out striker. To drop back and be expected to start spreading passes about wasn't something I was totally comfortable with and the cup final turned out to be one of my last first-team appearances that season.

I enjoyed picking up the cup-winner's medal, though, especially after the league-medal saga just a few months before. I did spare a thought for Peter McCloy when I got my hands on it. Peter played in every one of the nine League Cup ties leading up to the final, but missed out on the Hampden game through injury, and I had a part in that.

Either side of the final I played in two European Cup ties against Saint-Etienne, again in midfield. I'd played in the first round against Bohemia, but the French side were a very different proposition to the Irish, typically strong technically and well organised. They had won their league two years on the trot when we played them and went on to play Bayern Munich in the final of the European Cup after defeating us, losing 1–0 against the Germans. It was Bayern's third European Cup win in as many years, something that put our win over them on the road to Barcelona into perspective. The European Cup final in 1976 was played at Hampden and we set out on the European trail hoping it would lead us back to Glasgow. Unfortunately it wasn't to be.

The first leg over on the continent, just a few days before the cup final, was eventful to say the least. In the warm-up, I fired in a shot and Peter stuck a hand out to save it, breaking a finger in the process. He was carted away for treatment and Stewart Kennedy got the call at short notice to take over in goal. I went to see Peter in his room after the match, but he wouldn't open the door to me. He wasn't happy, obviously holding me responsible for the injury, and it took a while for the two of us to patch things up.

There was a lot of pressure on him at that time and he was still raw from sitting out the whole of the previous season, when Stewart had taken possession of the keeper's jersey. Having been around for so long, it must have hurt Peter to suddenly find himself on the sidelines for such an important season.

He regained his place at the start of the 1975/76 season, but that injury in St Etienne threatened to set him back to square one. To add insult to injury, I'd hit the shot with my left peg, my weaker foot, but obviously it still packed a punch when I caught the ball right. There was no intent on my part, but Peter wasn't in the mood to listen, so I left him alone.

We lost the first leg 2–0, a result that didn't do much to help Stewart Kennedy settle back into the team. Stewart was at his lowest ebb at that point, stemming from the infamous 5–1 defeat Scotland had suffered against England at Wembley in the summer of 1975.

Stewart was the keeper that day and took an absolute pasting in the press for his performance. Because Stewart, Colin Jackson, Derek Parlane, and Sandy Jardine were on international duty, they joined the Rangers tour of Australia late.

When Stewart arrived, you could tell by his body language that his confidence was shot to pieces. He was normally a jovial character, but he was down in the dumps. Jock Wallace came over to me on the training ground and said, 'Can you go over and gee up Stewart, you're better at that sort of thing than me.' I gave Jock some stick for that little admission, he was the boss after all, but did my best to pick him up. He'd actually started out with my local team, Linlithgow Rose, so I considered him one of my own.

He was a fantastic keeper, but that experience with Scotland really set him back. He was still just a young thing in goalkeeping terms, only 25 when he played at Wembley, but I don't know if he ever really got over it. Although he played a couple of games Down Under, Jock decided to start the season with Peter.

Having lost his place once, Peter was determined not to lose it again and began the campaign in good form. Until the injury in France, that is. He ended up spending two months on the sidelines recovering from it. Unfortunately for Stewart, three of the five defeats we suffered all season came during the spell he was back in the side and when Peter was available, he came straight back in.

By that time, I was parked on the sidelines. The second leg of the European Cup tie against St Etienne was my last appearance of the season, we lost 2–1 and went out of the competition. I didn't play badly, but after that Jock decided to revert to a more traditional approach and there was no room for me in the equation. It was the first time I'd been back in the European competition since the Barcelona final and I hadn't realised how much I'd missed it until I was involved again. It isn't just the football that is enjoyable, it's the whole sense of occasion.

I went from European football to the reserve league. While I was playing away in the second-team, the rest of the boys were on their way to another title. We won the Premier Division by six points, with Celtic runners-up, but with just six appearances I knew there was absolutely no chance of a medal again. The only difference was I couldn't argue about it this time, because I'd been a bit-part player.

It was a strange sensation watching it all unfold but being removed from it. I was always a Rangers supporter first and a player second, so from that point of view it was a time to celebrate. But as a professional, it was painful not to be more involved.

It was the same when we won the Scottish Cup final against Hearts to land the treble. Six months earlier, I'd been on the park at Hampden helping the team to the League Cup, but now all I could do was watch and cheer them on. I would have given anything to have been more involved in the treble, but for me it was a case of right place, wrong time.

19

Loan Ranger

I played against some world-class defenders in my time, everyone from Franz Beckenbauer to Bobby Moore. None of them caused me to lose any sleep and it wasn't one of those household names who convinced me my career was coming to an end, it was a forward called Martin Henderson. He didn't know it, but he was the one who persuaded me it was time to think seriously about the direction I was heading in. The name probably will not mean a lot to many people, but for one season Martin was the golden child, the apple of Jock Wallace's eye. With the best will in the world, he couldn't touch me as a goal scorer or as a player. Yet Martin Henderson was consistently chosen ahead of me the season after we won the league, and when that began to happen I knew I was in trouble.

Martin was just a kid when he was brought into the team by Jock but the big man must have seen something in him, something I just couldn't fathom. He was a teenager who had been brought through the youth ranks by Jock and parachuted straight into the first-team for the 1975/76 season. It wasn't just me that he leapfrogged, with Derek Parlane also falling behind him in the pecking order.

As I kicked my heels on a Saturday afternoon, he was out there wearing what had been my No. 9 shirt and I knew the game was just about up for me. Henderson turned out to be a one-season wonder, eventually loaned out to Hibs before moving on to America and then the lower leagues in England, but behind him there was a string of other young players scrambling to get a foothold at first-team level.

By the time the 1976/77 season rolled around, I was resigned to the fact that I was destined to spend it in the second string. I played a couple of Premier Division games towards the tail-end of 1976, one at Ibrox against Celtic and the other away to Hearts, but it was never going to be a permanent reprieve.

The fixture at Tynecastle turned out to be my last competitive match in the Rangers first-team. It fell on 26 November 1976 and we won 1–0, with Derek Parlane scoring the winner. At least I signed off on a high note, although the season itself wasn't one to remember for the club as we ended up without a trophy.

After the brief return to first-team duty, I reverted back to what had become my adopted role as the old head among the youngsters. While I was playing in the reserves, I had the pleasure of helping a few on their way who I thought had a real chance in the game. One in particular was Chris Robertson, the elder brother of the Hearts striker John Robertson. Chris did make the breakthrough while I was there, but never really established himself, which was a crying shame. He went on to play for Hearts and Meadowbank, amongst others, but I was sure he could have had more success than he did.

I spent the best part of a decade among seasoned old pros and, while I would have loved to still be with the first-team, the one benefit to dropping down to the reserves was the breath of fresh air the youngsters provided. They were all desperate to prove themselves and so keen to learn. None of them felt they knew it all and I was bowled over by their attitude. You couldn't help but get caught up in their enthusiasm and I found myself enjoying a second wind. For one thing, I had my reputation to protect, so I had to make sure I was the one leading by example. I like to think I did that and even although I had fallen out of the picture under Jock Wallace, I didn't let my standards slip and never gave anything less than my all during my time at Ibrox.

There was no fall-out with Jock and he appreciated the way I handled his decision to drop me into the reserves. When he saw the way I'd taken to it, he invited me to start helping out with coaching the side. It wasn't something I'd given much thought to, but the more I considered it, the more it appealed. I had a lot of experience to fall back on, in Scotland as well as in Europe and England, so it made sense to pass on what I could. Unfortunately, the idea didn't appeal quite as much to Joe Mason, who was in charge of the reserves at that time. He made it clear to Jock that he didn't want my help and that was the end of the idea before it got off the ground. I could see where Joe was coming from, because the last thing he needed was to be looking over his shoulder worrying about me taking his job further down the line, so the sensible thing for him was to nip it in the bud.

Joe had been brought to the club as a player from Morton, where he'd done a good job in the 1960s and early 1970s, before joining the coaching staff under big Jock. He'd come in just after I left for Coventry in 1972, so we were never teammates, but I got on well enough with him. In fact, I probably owe my good looks to him! There was a game down at Dumbarton where I took a bang to the face and went down needing treatment. There was a bit of blood, but I said I wanted to carry on until Joe came running on to drag me off, to save me from myself. It turned out that half my ear was hanging off and if he hadn't taken me away for treatment, I dread to think how it would have ended up.

Joe ended up losing out in the reshuffle when Jock came back to the club in the 1980s and was released, so maybe he was right to worry about his future when I was in the mix years earlier. For the record, I never had even the slightest thought in my mind about trying to edge him out of the picture and Jock never suggested it, either. I was only ever asked to lend a hand and unless I was told otherwise, that's all I would have done. It's not in my nature to go behind people's backs, but in football it's natural for the defences to go up, because it can be a ruthless game.

With that door closed on me, another unexpected one swung open when Willie Waddell called me into his office for a chat in October 1977. I'd been in and out of that room plenty of times in the past, but what he had to say this time wasn't exactly bad news. I had been out of the first-team for more than a year and knew my time at Ibrox was coming to an end. Despite that, I had kept myself in shape and the Deedle obviously felt I was good enough to do him one last favour.

Waddell was a legend at Kilmarnock after leading them to the league in 1965, and it turned out that he was still close to the board at Rugby Park. They turned to him when they were in trouble that year and he responded by parachuting me in on loan for the remainder of the season. As far as I'm aware, it didn't cost Killie a penny and Waddell made sure Rangers picked up the tab for my wages during the time I spent down there, so that his old club was looked after. He was basically managing them from afar, because I don't think for a minute they came looking for me in particular, Waddell made the decision for them on what they needed to get out of the difficult situation they were in.

It was a pleasant surprise for me, because it meant a return to competitive football after so long in the reserves. The structure of the deal was that I would continue to train at Ibrox through the week, but head down to Kilmarnock to work with them at their Thursday-night session. They held their midweek gatherings at Rugby Park where the referees also trained at the same time. I hadn't made too many friends amongst the men in black, to put it mildly, so I gave them a wide berth.

The circumstances of my move to Kilmarnock were far from ideal. I was brought in as cover following the death of Ian Fallis in a car crash. To say the mood was low would be an understatement, he'd been very popular at the club and with the supporters. He'd also been an effective player, their leading scorer when they won promotion from the First Division and again the following season in the Premier Division. The glory days under Waddell were not that far in the past, but they had become one of the country's yo-yo clubs and there was a feeling that they needed to stabilise and regroup.

Those goals weren't enough to keep Killie in the top-flight and they had toiled in amongst the big boys, dropping down again for the 1977/78 season. The glory days under Waddell were not that far in the past, but they had become one of the country's yo-yo clubs and there was a feeling that they needed to stabilise and regroup.

The death of Ian was traumatic for everyone at Killie and it came at around the same time as Willie Fernie quit as manager. It had been a horrible start to the season on and off the park, with not a single win from nine games by the time I was sent there on loan. That left them managerless and sitting twelfth in the 14-team First Division, hovering just above the two relegation places. Not surprisingly, there was a great deal of concern that things could go from bad to worse.

There was a delay in appointing a new man at the helm, with Davie Sneddon eventually getting the nod. Davie was a member of the championship-winning squad in 1965 and had been coaching the reserves under Fernie. He stepped up to steady the ship and made a decent fist of it, even if he wasn't the most charismatic manager I ever encountered. Davie took them back up to the Premier League the following season, although it did prove to be another short stay up there for the club.

My first game was at Rugby Park against Dumbarton, who challenged for promotion that season. I soon discovered that we had a cracking little squad in place and I got off to a scoring start in a 2–2 draw. As I knew from the past, a debut goal was as good a way of any of introducing yourself at a new club. Jim Stewart, our goalkeeper that day, is back at Rangers now as a coach and Stuart McLean, another great player from that era, still has a link to the SPL through his son Brian's place in the Falkirk squad.

Iain McCulloch, who would have run all day for the team,

was another key figure, and big Derrick McDicken also never gave in. Derrick was in the same mould as my old Coventry teammate Larry Lloyd – when you saw him galloping up from defence for a corner, you stood aside. Alan Robertson, a true Killie stalwart, was also going strong and Ian Jardine was another important player. Then there was a young winger by the name of Davie Provan, someone Scottish football would see a lot more of in the years ahead. Davie was a great wide player and it didn't take a genius to work out he had a bright future ahead of him.

After winning a point against Dumbarton, we were on the road again the following week for what was near enough a home game for me, at Alloa. I'd played a friendly at Recreation Park when I was with Armadale and it was a strange feeling to be back at one of the grounds where I'd first made my way in the game. A few years earlier, I'd been kicking back in the luxury of the Maracana Stadium and here I was squeezed into what has to be the smallest dressing room in football. We may as well have taken it in turns to get changed, it was that tight for space. Mind you, I had to get used to that claustrophobic feeling because the tunnel at Rugby Park was more like a crack in the wall. It must be the only place where teams have to run out individually because you can't get two players out the entrance side by side.

I had never played outside the top league, either in England or Scotland, so it was a new experience for me to drop down a level. It took me to a lot of different grounds and put me up against a clutch of new opponents. We were in the First Division with some big clubs, including Hearts and Morton, but there were also less fancied sides. East Fife, Stirling Albion, Queen of the South and Montrose were hardly big names, but I enjoyed the change of scene. The one disadvantage is that the heckling from the crowd is a whole lot clearer when there's a few hundred in the ground rather than 60,000. At Ibrox and Celtic Park, you're hit by noise and can barely make anything out; at Bayview and Links Park, you hear every shout and every jeer.

You need just as thick a skin to play in that type of environment as you do on the big stage.

Inside my first month or so with Killie we went up to Arbroath, my happy hunting ground from years gone by. Playing at Gayfield when it was packed with Rangers fans chanting my name was a far cry from going back and turning out in front of one man and his dog on a cold winter's afternoon. It was only nine years since I'd made my debut in light blue up there, but I'd travelled full circle.

Mind you, because of the bad winter that year I ended up playing in televised matches more than I had done for years. Rugby Park rarely falls victim to the weather, so while Premier Division games fell by the wayside, we played through the worst of it and received plenty of exposure into the bargain.

There was still some excitement in store, though, and it was the Scottish Cup that brought it that season. We edged past St Mirren in the first round and when the draw was made it may as well have been scripted Celtic at Celtic Park. I was going back into the lion's den to renew acquaintance with some old foes. Then the bad luck struck, I suffered a knock in the build-up to the tie and was told there was no way I would be fit to play. As my teammates went to Parkhead I stayed at home, having decided it would have been more hassle than it was worth to go along as a spectator. I never had a quiet time of it at Celtic, and sitting in the stand getting barracked by the home fans wasn't my idea of a good night out.

Celtic had lost five on the bounce in the league coming into the match but everyone, including them, expected us to get a bit of a going-over. We had a good squad together at Killie, but if I'm honest I didn't expect an upset. I couldn't believe it when I switched on the radio that evening and heard the result filtering through. Celtic's big centre-half Roddie MacDonald had scored but Donny McDowell, who scored a hatful of goals while I was playing alongside him that season, was also on target and it ended

1–1. Earning a replay was the jackpot for the club. For one thing, it meant another set of gate receipts and for another it allowed us a great shot at getting through to the next round on our own patch. To beat either of the Old Firm in Glasgow is nigh on impossible for the little teams, but if you can get them out of their comfort zone there's at least a fighting chance.

It was a stroke of luck for me, too, because it gave me the time to shake off the injury and put myself back in contention. The way the fixtures fell meant there was a three-week gap between the original tie and the replay, so I managed to squeeze in a couple of league games and was counting down to the Celtic match. I was enjoying playing week in and week out in the First Division, but missed the big matches and for me there was none bigger than the chance to get one over on Celtic. There was a big crowd squeezed into Rugby Park and a real buzz about the town, the result in the first tie had given everyone a lift.

By that time, Celtic had emerging young players like Roy Aitken, Pat McCluskey and Tommy Burns in the side and were full of running. But we had plenty of determination and experience to counter it and we gave as good as we got for the entire 90 minutes. Naturally, the Celtic supporters were on my back for the whole game, so there was nobody more delighted than me when Derrick McDicken headed home what proved to be the winner. The look on the big man's face was a picture and if anyone deserved his moment of glory, it was him. Derrick spent more than a decade at Kilmarnock and was a rough, tough Ayrshire boy who loved to get stuck in. Scoring the winner against Celtic in the Scottish Cup isn't a bad high- light for any player's CV and he enjoyed it right enough.

The noise when the ball hit the back of the net was fantastic and it was great for the players and the fans. Mind you, I couldn't indulge in the celebrations because I had the trek back to Linlithgow to contend with. When I returned to Rangers from Coventry, we moved back to our old patch, buying another house in the town, and put down roots once and for all. By then, we were planning for the future and knew that was where we wanted to be for the kids growing up. It meant an extra hour on the journey when I went out to Kilmarnock, but because I was still training at Ibrox it wasn't a problem – unless there was a big win to celebrate, of course. As it happened, I had a quick bottle of beer and then drove back up the road to leave the rest of them to it.

I received a hero's welcome when I went back to Ibrox after that, with the young boys at Rangers giving it laldy when I walked in. I didn't know there were so many Kilmarnock fans in Govan! That welcome didn't last too long, mind you. When the draw for the quarter-finals was announced, Killie were pulled from the hat with Rangers, at Ibrox, and the fun really began.

I'd been sent to Coventry once before by the club and it happened again that day. Jock Wallace came looking for me straight away and told me I was banned from training with them. The reserves and the first-team would mix things up through the course of the week, particularly for practice games, and he claimed I'd be in on too many tactical secrets to be able to carry on working with them in the build-up to the tie. Not for the first time, I tried to argue my case but he was having none of it. I was barred and that was that. Fortunately, it didn't last too long, with the delay for the previous tie meaning that there was only a short wait for the quarter-final matches to be played.

I suppose it might have been worse and Rangers could have tried to block me from playing against them altogether, but there was never any suggestion of that. Loans were far less common in those days and clubs weren't as precious about the guys they sent out on temporary deals. As far as they were concerned, I was a Killie player for the rest of the season and it was up to Davie Sneddon to decide where my loyalties lay.

There was never any doubt in my mind. I wanted to play and if there was a chance to win it for Kilmarnock, I would have done it. I remember Derek Johnstone was in the same position when he came up on loan to Dundee United from Chelsea and he felt exactly the same way, you owe it to the team you're playing for to give it your all, no matter who you are up against.

Rangers were always going to be a different proposition to Celtic, who had been toiling in the Premier Division. Jock had the boys flying that year and they had been leading the league since October. When we played them in March, they already had the League Cup in the cabinet and were stick-ons for the title, too. They were on a mission to win another treble and that day we just didn't have an answer to them.

The men who were my colleagues through the week suddenly became the opposition and I had to turn left to the away dressing room instead of following autopilot in the other direction to the home side. Jock took no chances whatsoever and put out his strongest team.

That included John Greig at left back and I was sure that gave us a chance. John was no spring chicken by then and it turned out to be his final season before taking over as manager a few months later. Like myself, he had lost a bit of pace and with a young Davie Provan going up against him I thought it represented a great opportunity to get in behind them. I pulled Davie to one side before we went out and told him to run at Greigy at every opportunity. He did and John promptly whacked him, just the same way as he had Szabo in the Barcelona final. Davie barely kicked another ball and had to be substituted; so much for my grand plan.

My own head-to-head was with Tom Forsyth, someone I'd had what you might call a few differences of opinion with while he was with Motherwell and I was with Rangers. We were hardly the best of friends after he moved to Ibrox, but I never got much chance to try my luck against him that day because we were pegged back for most of the game. We hadn't set out to defend, but the boys in light blue were pretty formidable and it became a case of damage limitation not long into the match.

Gordon Smith and Derek Johnstone were a strong partnership up front and it was DJ who settled the home side's nerves when he scored early on. Johnny Hamilton, John MacDonald and Davie Cooper made it four and although we clawed back a consolation through Iain McCulloch, the result was never in doubt. Rangers beat Dundee United in the semi-final before getting the better of Aberdeen in the final to complete the treble.

The result was disappointing from a Kilmarnock perspective, but for me it was a mixed afternoon. The reception I received from the Rangers supporters, even though I was on the opposition team, was fantastic and it really warmed my heart. They hadn't forgotten me and that meant a lot to me, as it always had done. When you win a place in their affections, you tend never to lose it. I can't explain why that happened for me, all I know is that it has given me enormous pleasure and pride over the years.

The cup run kept the interest in our season bubbling away nicely and it coincided with a lift in league form. In my time at Killie, we moved from twelfth to finish the campaign in sixth, not promotion-winning material but an awful lot better than fighting relegation as we were in the early days. It was Morton, under Benny Rooney, who won the league on goal difference from Willie Ormond's Hearts side, but at least Killie were back on the right road.

We went on a fair old run in the time I was at the club and it struck me as time went on that I hadn't received a single win bonus. I knocked on Willie Waddell's door and queried it with him. Without hesitation he said he'd get it sorted out and he was true to his word. From then on, my pay packets were adjusted accordingly.

I put together a good spell of games, playing 23 in a row after joining them, and produced a decent return with eight goals in

the First Division. It dispelled in my own mind the fears that my
body wasn't up to the rigours of football at a decent level, but
was not enough to convince me that I still had a future in the
game. I knew the time would come when I would have a
decision to make.

20

Out of the blue

The phone rang and I answered it to a familiar voice. It was Jock Wallace and he didn't take long to cut to the chase. He said, 'I'm giving you a free transfer.' All I could think to say was, 'Thanks, boss', and that was that. My life as a Rangers player was over, and within weeks I called time on my career as a footballer.

It was the summer of 1978 and I had not long turned 31. If I'd wanted to, I could probably have had another five or six years in the game, but after a lot of soul-searching I decided I just couldn't go on. I would have been cheating myself and whoever employed me, because my heart wasn't in it any longer.

The first seeds of doubt had been sown when I first lost my place in the Rangers top team. I'd grown up on a diet of success and the rush of scoring goals in front of massive crowds. I knew when I dropped out of the team at Ibrox that those days were behind me and I would have to settle for something less, something on a smaller scale.

I enjoyed playing at Kilmarnock, but it was no substitute for what I had savoured as a Rangers player. Then there was the unseemly side of life in the lower leagues, the threats and the abuse. In many ways, it was worse as a Killie player than it was as an Old Firm star.

Because I was high-profile and a big name, I found myself becoming a target for every madman and would-be Chopper Harris in the division. They'd seek me out before a ball had been kicked, telling me they were going to break my legs, snap me in two and all the rest.

I'd seen and heard it all before, not least when we played lower leagues clubs with Coventry, because those sides in England all had a man-mountain in their defence. It seemed to be compulsory down there, and they could do some damage if you gave them half a chance.

That was fine when I was on the way up, when there were big prizes on the line. The question I had to ask myself was whether or not it was worth it on the way down, when really I was playing the game because I loved it and not for any other reason. Did I want to spend my Saturday afternoons having to fend off the attention of guys who obviously felt the only way they could make a name for themselves was to be the one who broke Colin Stein's leg?

They never did manage it, I was too streetwise for them and could still handle myself. But I wasn't a boxer, I didn't want every game to be a sparring match, and the whole attitude I'd found lower down the leagues just didn't sit right for me. I always loved a battle on the park but this was different, it wasn't about football. I had a couple of options to consider at home and abroad, but it didn't take me long to decide it was time to walk away from football.

Davie White, who had been so supportive when I first joined Rangers, was still looking out for me. He had contacts in Australia and he alerted them to my availability while I was still at Kilmarnock, obviously guessing that my contract wouldn't be extended by Jock.

It was a Queensland club who sent a scout to watch me and they saw enough to pursue the possibility of taking me Down Under. Plenty of people were heading to America at that time, but fewer had tested the water in Australia and it was something that turned my head. Having been on the tour of the country with Rangers just a few years earlier, I knew the quality of life out there was high, but I also knew the standard of football wasn't on a par with our own leagues. It would have been a good environment to bring up the kids in, but on the other hand it would have meant taking them away from family and friends.

Linda and I weighed things up but really I'd already made my mind up to retire and I wouldn't go back on it. It would have either involved uprooting the family again or an incredible amount of travelling, and neither was ideal. I've never regretted the decision not to go because I don't think it would have been a switch for life and as I moved into my 30s, I had to look to the future.

The other call I took around the same time came from closer to home and from a more familiar voice. It was Dave Smith, asking me to join him at Berwick Rangers. Dave had taken over as manager at Shielfield a couple of years previously and was putting together a good side, with Willie Mathieson working beside him. The squad was part-time and training sessions were in Edinburgh, so it would have been ideal in many ways. It was tempting to work with those two and if I had, I would have won a Second Division championship medal the following season, but I let my head rule my heart and stuck to my guns. I was done with football.

The last team to try their luck in tempting me back was my home-town team, Linlithgow Rose. Davie Roy, the man who rejected me as a teenager, came calling, but I said, 'Davie, if I wasn't good enough all those years ago, I'm not good enough for you now.' I guess they thought it was worth a try, but the prospect of going back to the juniors was never a viable one. If it had been bad in the First Division as far as defenders trying to make a name for themselves, imagine what it would have been like outside the senior leagues.

There were a few other nibbles from teams in Scotland, but I didn't actively look for alternatives and eventually the phone stopped ringing. Football's a small industry and people soon got the message that my mind was made up. I'd kicked my last ball, and scored my last goal.

I decided on a clean break from the game. If I'm being honest, I was disillusioned by the way it had turned out for me. I was still physically fit, even if I wasn't at my peak, and I hadn't lost my instinct or my ability to sniff out chances. I'm a great believer that you can't teach goal-scoring and also that it's a knack that never deserts you. Yet by the time I turned 30, I was effectively out of the picture at Rangers and sent out to pasture.

It was a difficult thing to get my head round. When you are playing you never believe it will end, you think it's all about champagne and silverware. Then in an instant it is gone. My whole adult life had been built around football and suddenly that part of me was gone. I wasn't bitter about the fact I was starting afresh, but I guess I'd fallen out of love with football, for the first time it just didn't matter to me any more.

When I turned my back on it, I walked straight into a job as a car salesman. I'd been in the motor trade before, when I went into partnership with a businessman called John Kerr not long after joining Rangers in the late 1960s. We opened up Colin Stein Garages on Paisley Road West, on the corner of Dumbreck Road, selling used cars and doing repairs. We went our separate ways when I moved to England, but John's still trading on Portman Road, not far from where our place was.

When I went back into the car business in 1978, it was purely short-term, an offer that was there for me at the right time but not one that had me hooked, and I knew there would be something more suited to me around the corner. I'd taken a break after deciding to retire, time to clear my head and work out what was next for me, and then took up the job offer. But it wasn't me. I just couldn't imagine seeing out my days as a salesman, so I went back to my roots. I had my trade as a joiner and that was something I felt more enthusiastic about pursuing, so I got myself a job and threw myself back into it.

The response was mixed. Some people didn't bat an eyelid, others were excited to have me around and a handful made it clear they felt I shouldn't be there, for no other reason than that I was Colin Stein. I couldn't follow that logic; like everyone else I needed to work, not just to put money in the bank, but to stay busy and use the skills I had. When I completed my apprenticeship in the 1960s I knew I had a career in football ahead of me, but I finished it because I always intended to go back into joinery. For more than a quarter of a century, I've been working away in the trade and I still go into work with a smile on my face. I count myself very lucky.

For five years I didn't set foot back inside Ibrox, didn't watch any football and really didn't pay any attention. Then, out of the blue, the phone rang and I answered it to a familiar voice. It was Jock Wallace and, as always, he didn't take long to cut to the chase. He said, 'I want you to come back to Ibrox.' Again, all I could think to say was, 'Thanks, boss.' Jock was not long back at the club himself, having been drafted in when John Greig resigned in 1983. He was restructuring the coaching set-up and part of that included the youth teams. I was invited to start working with the under-16 side and all of a sudden the spark was back. I'd fallen in love with football again.

The man who helped me to do that was Bobby Dinnie. He was the quietest, most gentle man I ever met, but underneath that he had a phenomenal ability to spot a football player. Bobby turned Possil YM into a feeder club for some of the giants in English football and he eventually linked up with Rangers, bringing some wonderful youngsters to Ibrox. He was awarded an MBE in 1998 and anyone who has ever met the man would tell you that was a fitting reward.

It was Bobby who put the team together that I took under my wing and we went on to have success, winning the Scottish Cup and a few other trophies along the way. We played at Tinto Park, the home of Benburb juniors, and worked hard to make a go of it. The kids gave me tremendous respect from day one and it was a humbling experience. Every minute I spent on the

training field with them, pounding the ash parks, was a pleasure.
The only down side was the reaction you got when you took a
Rangers team on the road. You can dress it up as jealousy, but all
I could see was hatred. I'll always remember one particular
Glasgow league game in Motherwell where we met the type of
vitriol from opposition parents that I'd never experienced in my
life. I can't fathom the mentality of people who can stand and
hurl abuse at boys who are just trying to learn the game, but I'll
bet it is still going on now. What I do know is that type of
treatment just makes those wearing the Rangers badge on their
chest fight even stronger for the cause, and it was character-
building for the kids in that side.

I would have loved to stay alongside them through their
apprenticeships with the club, but unfortunately it wasn't to be.
Jock brought in two additional youth coaches he had worked
with at Motherwell, both teachers, and I just couldn't click with
them. It came to a head when they sat the boys down and started
lecturing them like they were in a classroom. It reminded me of
the way I'd been spoken to as a schoolboy and I didn't agree
with it. They were with us to become better football players, not
be talked down to and patronised. It was totally at odds with the
way I wanted to do things, so I took them into the tunnel at
Ibrox, hammered them at head tennis, two against one, and then
walked off into the sunset. I left behind a great group of boys
who kept in touch with me long after, and they knew I was
always there to lend an ear or offer advice, even if it was in an
unofficial capacity.

None of them made it big with Rangers, but that's just typical
of the way it has been for generations at the Old Firm. Those
who do come through the ranks are very much the exceptions
rather than the rule, because the pressure on every manager to
deliver instant success is enormous and there isn't the scope to
take a gamble with untried players.

It was not long after I had been involved that the David

Murray era began and from that moment in time, it was virtually impossible for a Rangers youth team player to progress. The money flooded in and the team was packed with big name signings. I can understand why it has been done that way for years, but I do wonder how many great young players have fallen by the wayside because of the reliance on experience over youth.

It is more than 25 years since I left the Rangers coaching staff and I have often wondered if I should have gone back for a second bite at it. I've watched a lot of my former teammates do great things in management, not least Tommy McLean with Motherwell and Alex MacDonald with Hearts and Airdrie, and with glorious hindsight it would have been interesting to test myself in that line of work. At the time I didn't do my coaching badges, so I fell off the radar. If you do that, there's no way back.

I certainly didn't pine for football after my time with the youths, it wasn't really until the Barcelona team started getting together again for reunions that I began to get more involved again. James Mortimer brought us together at Victoria's nightclub in Glasgow in 1992 for the twentieth anniversary and since then we've had regular squad gatherings, including a trip to Canada with the club to attend the North American Rangers Supporters Association conference and a pilgrimage back to the Camp Nou in 2007 when the club was on European duty. We now all appreciate just what we achieved in 1972 and what we had as a team, which was a special group of players and characters. Aside from the reunions, quite a few of us are now back working for Rangers on match days at Bar 72 and the other function suites. I enjoy being involved on the hospitality side, it keeps a link not just with the club but with my old teammates and the supporters. I'm fortunate that all of my former clubs try to keep the ex-pros involved, from the legends days at Coventry to the former players' club that has been started up at Hibs. I'm a member of the Hibs group and plan to attend a few of the meetings when I get the chance.

I watch games here and there, but to be honest there's no substitute for playing. When I packed in football I had to look elsewhere for the competitive buzz. I've always had a love for sport in all shapes and forms. My golf was a big passion and I became a pretty handy table tennis player during my time at Ibrox.

Bowls is another game I dabbled in while I was still playing football and after I retired I was able to take it up more seriously. Linlithgow Bowling Club was just a stone's throw from our house at that time, and I was soon hooked. In fact, I still am.

I retired from football in 1978 and won the bowling club championship that summer. I've won it another five times since then, so my titles span four different decades, from the 1970s right through to my most recent one in 2005. Hopefully it won't be my last and I'm still playing, as well as managing my county side, West Lothian. We've traditionally had a strong team and there are a lot of talented players on our patch. We last won the Hamilton Trophy, the sport's equivalent of the Scottish Cup, in 1997 but if we play to our potential, it won't be long until it's back with us again.

The great thing is that bowling became a family affair. Linda took up the game and was secretary at the club for a spell, while both of the kids also really got into it and have played at a high level, with Nicola representing Scotland and Martin following in my footsteps by winning the Linlithgow championship.

A lot of people find it difficult to imagine me as a bowler, because they remember me as an all-action football player, but I'm in my element when I'm on the green. It's not an easy game, you need a good eye for it, and the competitive element suits me. The other side of the coin is that it's a really sociable sport and there's far more to it than just the organised games, so you get the best of both worlds.

Managing the county team as well as competing keeps me busy. At the height of the season, I'll be playing every night of the week and then have the county fixtures on a Saturday and the under-25 team to look after on a Sunday. It takes up a lot of my time, but it's a pleasure not a chore. I've had a lot of fun over the years through the game.

The most important thing has always been the family involvement. When I retired from football, Nicola was still only eight and Martin just five. Linda had done a wonderful job bringing them up. As any footballer's wife will tell you, it can be a difficult life at times. I spent an awful lot of time away from home, whether it was playing in Europe or on the long summer tours, and it wouldn't have been possible without Linda's support. Everyone looks at the glamorous side of life in football, and while I wouldn't swap my career for anyone else's, there are sacrifices which have to be made and those mainly impact on your family.

The best decision I ever made was marrying Linda. She's been there to encourage me when I've needed it or to keep my feet on the ground. She is a wonderful wife and mother. The fact that the children were still young when I hung up my boots meant I didn't miss them growing up altogether and while it would have been nice for them to have seen me at my peak, I'm grateful that I was able to spend more time with them once I'd stopped playing.

I could talk all day about what I've done in football, but my family is by far my proudest achievement. Nicola and her husband, Steven, have a son and a daughter, Emma and Jack, while Martin and his wife, Dianne, have their boys, Ethan and Cole. The four grandkids are the apple of our eyes and watching them grow and become their own personalities is brilliant, nobody can make me smile the way they can. I'm so proud of each of them and because both Martin and Nicola live in Linlithgow, we see plenty of them.

We're a close family, even more so since recent events. Nicola was diagnosed with breast cancer, but thankfully has now received the all-clear after a long period of treatment. It was a terrible time, but she was so strong and that gave us courage. I would have swapped places with her in an instant if I could have. Something like that puts everything in perspective, from the biggest thing to the smallest. I was sitting at home one night puffing away on my pipe, as I have done for as long as I can remember, when I suddenly thought, 'What am I doing, my daughter's fighting cancer and I'm doing this to myself.' I put the pipe away that night and it won't be lit again. More than ever, I appreciate all the good things in my life.

Only Martin, who followed me into the joinery trade, and Nicola, who has built a career as a medical secretary at the Royal Hospital For Sick Children in Edinburgh, can say what it meant to grow up as Colin Stein's children. Because we never strayed from our friends and family in West Lothian, I don't think it was too big a factor for them, although Martin probably had a bit more weight on his shoulders because of his dad.

He was a very useful young football player before injuries struck, but because of the Stein factor people probably looked at him differently. I suppose it was only natural for others to compare him to me. That couldn't have been easy, but both he and his sister have made their own way in the world and done us proud. We couldn't have wished for better kids.

21

Looking to the future

Through all the highs and lows of life in football, more often than not it all comes back to one event: Barcelona. I was fortunate to achieve many things and savour some wonderful occasions throughout my career, but what we achieved that night in 1972 remains the highlight. I knew it was special then, but with every passing year I grow to appreciate it even more.

For any Scotsman, running out at Hampden in front of more than 100,000 members of the Tartan Army is an amazing feeling. But it cannot eclipse the pure joy we felt that night in Spain. When I played against England at Wembley, it was another dream come true. But Barcelona trumped it. Partnering Denis Law in attack made me feel like a kid in a sweetie shop, but it was still just shaded by the events of 1972. Scoring the goal that ended Celtic's league domination was a massive thrill, but nowhere close to scoring at the Camp Nou.

The question I get asked more often than any other is whether or not our achievement will ever be matched – can Rangers win again in Europe? The short answer is, yes. Anything is possible in football, but it will not be easy for the club to earn another prize at the highest level and it will take everyone pulling in the right direction to even get close.

As the rich get richer and the Scottish teams get left behind, the Champions League is slipping further and further from the realms of possibility for both halves of the Old Firm. It saddens me to see any team celebrating reaching the last 16 of a competition, but that is probably as good as it will get for

Rangers and Celtic. I maintain Rangers are as big as any club in Europe, but in financial terms they are dwarfed by scores of teams from the wealthiest leagues. Because of that, it is nearly impossible to compete.

That does not mean it has to be all doom and gloom though. We saw when Rangers reached the Uefa Cup final in 2008 just what is possible and for that reason alone, fans are entitled to dream about what the future might hold. During that run to Manchester, the manager got it spot on. He may have been pilloried for the one-up-front game plan, but nobody can argue with the results Walter Smith achieved in Europe that season.

My only disappointment was that, having reached the final and done the hard part, Walter didn't throw caution to the wind in the final and have a go at Zenit. Once you reach that stage, there should be no fear and the shackles have to come off. It should be like two boxers slugging it out toe-to-toe in the middle of the ring, not one sitting back on the ropes from the first bell.

On the eve of the 2008 final, I had an STV crew in my living room filming a preview piece. I was asked if the Rangers team for that match could expect to become legends if they won. The very fact that I was there with the television cameras in my house 36 years after Barcelona answered the question.

Many wonderful players have passed through Ibrox over the years and achieved great things, but only the 1972 squad have gone that extra mile and won a European trophy. It humbles me to think of the greats over the years who cannot lay claim to that achievement, and I am proud that I am part of the squad that did it.

We still talk about Barcelona and the interest in Aberdeen's squad from Gothenburg in 1983 and the Lisbon Lions is as strong as it has ever been. If Rangers had won that night in Manchester, there would have been a new set of legends for the TV companies to seek out.

The line between fame and immortality is very fine, but I believe that the Barca Bears will never be forgotten. Each member of the team is now in the Rangers hall of fame and it still sends a shiver down my spine to walk up the marble staircase and see all of our names up there on the board. Nobody can take away from us the part we played in the history of our club.

I don't know how the team who ran out in Manchester felt about our presence hanging over them. Maybe they never gave it a second thought, but I would imagine some must be sick of hearing about 1972. The only way they can put that right is by winning in Europe again and creating their own slice of history.

More than anyone else, that would make the chairman happy. David Murray has ploughed something in the region of £80 million in transfer fees into trying to emulate what we achieved and I can understand his frustration at not managing it. There's maybe even a touch of resentment about it because there are constant reminders from the glory days.

My own view is that throwing money blindly at the squad was always the wrong approach, or at least it was when it was carried out in recent years. The £12 million spent on Tore Andre Flo was the final straw, a catastrophic piece of business. Flo just did not look like a Rangers centre-forward and I felt sorry for him. There was no doubt he was a decent player, but he shouldn't have been put in the position of carrying the hopes of the entire Rangers support, because he just wasn't up to it.

Then there was Egil Ostenstad. Anyone could have told you that he wasn't the answer, yet there he was in a Rangers shirt hoovering up obscene amounts of money for the pleasure of doing next to nothing on park. Or how about Nuno Capucho? A man so out of shape when he arrived at Ibrox that I would have fancied my chances in a race against him, and I'm in my 60s.

One by one, these signings have trickled into Ibrox and more often than not disappeared with their tail between their legs but with their bank account bulging. It really hurts me to see players using Rangers as a cash cow, with no feeling for the traditions the likes of Bill Struth fought so hard to establish.

With the current financial problems facing every industry, there may actually be a chance for Rangers to put right the wrongs of recent years. They will have to look closer to home for bargains and that should push them back in the direction of young Scottish talent. The club's policy of cherry-picking the best players from their opponents took me from Easter Road to Ibrox and it is one they would be well advised to revisit. No matter how badly off the Old Firm teams are, the rest will be in a worse position financially. There is always the opportunity to pick up some bargains.

We don't want to go back to the days when a player would have signing forms waved under their nose in the car park if they had as much as one good game against Rangers, but there has to be a greater emphasis on bringing in people who know what the club is about and can relate to the pressures that are associated with Old Firm life.

Craig Levein at Dundee United has been able to unearth some real gems from the lower leagues, down as far as the Third Division, and I firmly believe the future will be bright for the clubs who take it upon themselves to delve into every corner in the search for fresh blood.

Walter Smith is a very shrewd manager and the right man to lead Rangers forward. Walter is so adept at choosing a shape to fit the players he has at his disposal, rather than trying to shoehorn his team into a formation that just doesn't work for them. I hope Walter is given a decent length of time to continue moulding his team because there are signs of green shoots, as the championship win in 2009 proved.

The judgement will always be made on European results and if the run to the final in Manchester proved anything, it was that you do not always need the best players in the world to make progress. With the right organisation and motivation, there could be some more great European nights at Ibrox to enjoy.

Key to making strides in the right direction will be keeping Kris Boyd happy and content. I cannot for the life of me understand the criticism Kris comes in for. People want him to be more involved in games, but you can't run down the wing, cross it and get on the end of the ball yourself. Every team needs a poacher and Rangers can afford to let him do what he is best at and forget the rest. Boyd is a born goal-scorer and it would be foolish to surrender that and let him move on. Okay, so he doesn't always put in a back-breaking shift, but Alistair McCoist was hardly a worker ant and it didn't do him any harm.

I would have Kris Boyd in my team every day of the week and the way he was treated by George Burley is nothing short of disgraceful. He's taken pelters for turning his back on his country, but in reality he'd already had the door slammed in his face when he was left sitting on the bench for the World Cup qualifier against Norway at Hampden in 2008. It was a game crying out for Boyd's scoring instinct, but instead we had James McFadden playing up front on his own, a position my eight-year-old granddaughter could tell you just doesn't suit McFadden.

At 0–0 the stage was set for Boyd to shake things up. Instead we got Chris Iwelumo. To say Kris walked away is twisting things slightly – you would have to be picked first and he wasn't getting a sniff. That decision against the Norwegians summed up George Burley for me, it seemed senseless. I'm far from convinced Burley is the right man for the top job and his decision to take Terry Butcher, the proudest Englishman you could ever meet, on board doesn't sit right. Having Steven Pressley on the staff, a man with no management experience when he was appointed as a Scotland coach, defied belief. The whole regime appears out of kilter.

I am immensely proud to have played my part for my country and dearly want to see us back competing at the level we deserve. Unfortunately, as long as Burley is in charge and continues to alienate our best players, we don't stand much of a chance.

The treatment of Barry Ferguson and Allan McGregor in 2009 was terrible. Had Burley acted properly and sent the pair of them home as soon as their indiscretions became clear, it would never have escalated to the stage it is at now. Scotland are not in the position to be handing out lifetime bans to any international players, let alone two who could have been very useful in the years ahead.

Surely it could have been dealt with a lot more sensitively and without the media circus which surrounded it, but that isn't the way things are done by the SFA at the moment. It was all press statements and television appearances, with the various people from the association tying themselves in knots as they tried to explain their way out of what should have been no more than a storm in a teacup.

I've always felt football can get overcomplicated at times. It's a simple game if it is done properly, on and off the park, and if you cut through the bluster, all that matters is ability and application.

If I rattled off my all-time greatest Rangers team, it wouldn't have 11 saints in it but it would be a team that would give any other side a run for its money. I'd go for Andy Goram in goal, because he has to be the greatest shot-stopper Scottish football has ever seen. Then I'd plump for Sandy Jardine, Eric Caldow, Ronnie McKinnon, Jim Baxter and John Greig with Willie Henderson, Paul Gascoigne and Brian Laudrup providing the creativity and Willie Johnston and Derek Johnstone at the sharp end. Bud never did get the chance to play through the middle with DJ and that was a chance missed, because the pair of them would have been a revelation.

Choosing John Greig and Jim Baxter needs no explanation

and I've always made my admiration of Ronnie McKinnon clear. He was a nightmare to play against and a joy to have on your side. Eric Caldow would tell you he's the best left-back Ibrox has ever seen and he'd be right. Which is why he gets my vote, and with Sandy on the other side of the defence you would have a well-balanced full-back partnership. Sandy got better and better with every passing season and possessed all the attributes a modern right-back needs. With Henderson on one wing and Laudrup on the other, two players who could beat a man for fun, you would be assured the strikers would get service all day long, especially with Gascoigne and Baxter's creativity and inventiveness. Both Gazza and Slim had their demons to fight, but maybe that's what gave them the edge on the park.

If you look at that group of 11 players, what you find above all else is personality. That's the ingredient I think Scottish football lacks at present, but hopefully that will change in time. I try not to look back through rose-tinted glasses at my playing days, but sometimes I have to remind myself that Scotland was a nation packed with genuinely world-class players at that time.

Somewhere between then and now we have lost our way, but I do feel we can get back to being a successful football nation, both in club and international terms. I'd give anything to be able to turn back the clock and pull my boots on again, but I've had my turn and I loved it. Every goal and every game was a pleasure and my only advice to the next generation is to enjoy it while it lasts. You just never know when it will come to an end.

Index

Davis, Harold 93, 174
Davis, Joe 159
Delfin Playa Hotel 42
Dennison, Bob 154
Denny, Jim 135
Devonshire Arms, Coventry 152
Dickson, Billy 61
Dinnie, Bobby 205–6
Docherty, Tommy 79–81, 82, 83, 84, 85
Dorothy (sister) 15
Dumbarton FC 181, 191, 193
Duncan, Bobby 31, 33, 74
Dundalk 45, 51, 52, 53
Dundas Hotel 32
Dundee FC 28, 35, 116, 135, 169
Dundee United FC 65, 102, 169, 171, 198, 199, 214
Dunfermline FC 94, 143–4, 181
Dynamo Berlin 122

East Fife FC 35, 194
East Stirling FC 15, 16
Easter Road Lane 30
Easter Road Stadium 1, 2, 4, 7, 8, 17, 24, 27–31, 33, 35, 37, 45, 50, 51
  Shed at 30
Edinburgh 7, 9, 11, 18, 28, 31, 32, 39
  derby games in 30
  Princes Street 4, 5
  Queen Street 40
Edvaldsson, Johannes 185
Elland Road, Leeds 34
England 6, 8, 17, 22, 25, 77, 141
  infamous 5–0 defeat at Wembley 186–7
  at Wembley 14, 72–4, 85, 149, 150–51, 211
Eskisehirspor 122
Estrekov, Vladimir 126
Europe 29, 53, 54

European Championship 33, 84
European Cup 28, 185–6
  semi-final defeat for Celtic (1972) 117–18
European Cup-Winners Cup 23, 64, 80, 87, 88, 136, 140
  defeat in final (1967) 132
  Dynamo Moscow final in Barcelona (1972) 119–29
  line up for final in Barcelona (1972) 124, 130–35
  medal presentation (low key) and celebrations on win in Barcelona 127–9
  Rennes to Bayern Munich (1971/72) 105–18
  supporters, dedication of 121, 124, 125, 127, 128
Eusebio 83
Everton FC 5, 6, 8, 39, 145

FA Cup 5
Fairgrieve, John 112
Fairs Cup 32, 34, 45, 53, 87
  with Hibernian in 1967/8 season 32–3
  semi-final defeat 63–4
Falkirk FC 31, 35, 193
Fallis, Ian 192–3
Fallon, Sean 185
Ferguson, Alex 9, 10, 11, 37, 38, 45, 52, 56, 65
Ferguson, Barry 216
Ferguson, Margaret (Ibrox disaster victim) 99, 101
Fernie, Willie 193
Finham, Coventry Golf Club in 25–6
Finney, Sir Tom 150
Firhill Stadium 24
First Division 9, 15, 17, 24, 31, 34, 44, 54
Flo, Tore Andre 213